HAROLD K. MAWELA

# WORK SMART NOT HARD

## BREAKING HABITS THAT ARE STEALING YOUR TIME

ISBN: 9781795882071

This ebook was created with StreetLib Write
 http://write.streetlib.com

# Table of contents

| | |
|---|---|
| ACKNOWLEDGMENTS | 4 |
| INTRODUCTION | 5 |
| PART 1: PRODUCTIVITY | 8 |
|    THE CHANGING ENVIRONMENT | 9 |
|    UNDERSTANDING TIME MANAGEMENT | 15 |
|    PLANNING | 23 |
|    SHAPING YOUR FUTURE WITH GOALS | 33 |
|    CONVERTING PLANS INTO ACHIEVEMENTS | 39 |
|    MANAGING TECHNOLOGY | 49 |
|    EMAIL | 55 |
|    KEEP YOUR LIFE IN BALANCE | 61 |
| PART 2: HOW TO ORGANIZE | 67 |
|    TIME MANAGEMENT & ORGANIZATION | 68 |
|    GET ORGANIZED | 75 |
|    HOW ORGANIZED IS YOUR OFFICE? | 81 |
|    MERGING TIME & ORGANIZATION | 94 |
|    ORGANIZING YOUR HOME | 102 |
|    ORGANIZING YOUR HOME CAN BE FUN | 109 |
|    EVERYTHING I KNOW | 116 |
|    GAINING CONTROL | 120 |

## PART 3: KEEP YOUR BALANCE — 126
- BALANCE — 127
- DON'T BECOME A WORKAHOLIC — 129
- MAINTAINING BALANCE IN YOUR LIFE — 133
- JUGGLING CAREER, HOME AND FAMILY — 139
- SIMPLIFYING YOUR LIFE — 144
- SIMPLIFYING WHAT YOU DO — 150
- THE ROLE OF MINDFULNESS IN LIFE BALANCE — 155

## PART 4: USE YOUR ENERGY TO FULL EFFECT — 161
- IF ONLY IT WERE THIS SIMPLE... — 162
- SELF MANAGEMENT — 163
- PROCRASTINATION — 173
- IT'S ALL ABOUT ENERGY AND WILL POWER — 177
- HOW TO SET PRIORITIES — 199
- SYSTEMS IN SHORT — 203
- SPECIFIC AREAS — 209

## PART 5: MAKING TECHNOLOGY WORK FOR YOU — 219
- THE USE OF TECHNOLOGY — 220
- RUNNING OUT OF TIME? — 229
- DEPLETED BY TECHNOLOGY — 232
- HOW TO MANAGE TECHNOLOGY — 236
- MULTITASKING — 241
- TIME STRATEGY — 244
- CONTROL YOUR BRAIN — 248

ABOUT THE AUTHOR — 253

# WORK SMART NOT HARD

## BREAKING HABITS THAT ARE STEALING YOUR TIME

HAROLD K. MAWELA

Copyright © 2019 by (HAROLD K. MAWELA)

All rights reserved. No part of this book may be reproduced or transmitted any form or by any means without written permission from the author.

harold.mawela@gmail.com

https://www.facebook.com/ haroldleadership/

http:// haroldkmawelaover- blog.com/

https:// mobile.twitter.com/ haroldmawela? p=s

# ACKNOWLEDGMENTS

A book is never the result of just one person. I'd like to thank God.." Thanks to My father / Mentor / Spiritual father Apostle SM Mawela for reminding me of my purpose my mother MM Mawela she is a pillar indeed and to the entire Mawela family you are a great nation. AFM Word of faith,AFM Akasia family and AFM GNN Region thank you for helping me to discover my gifts it is an honor to serve you. And last but perhaps most important, thanks to my family, my wife Zanele my Kids Maatla, Seetsa and Botlalo who did without me while I spent countless hours at the computer, in the library, and in my "study" digesting and merging leadership wisdom. You provide my inspiration and purpose.

# INTRODUCTION

People have always searched for better and more efficient ways of doing things, whether it involved a more effective way of trapping animals for food or a more efficient way of starting a fire with friction. But it wasn't until the later 1800s and early 1900s that anyone took a purposeful, scientific approach to getting things done faster with less effort. Frederick Winslow Taylor is normally considered to be the father of scientific management. He wrote his book, *The Principles of Scientific Management* in 1911, which, together with the work of Frank and Lillian Gilbreth, became the launching pad for today's time management. It started as a quest to increase productivity in manufacturing, focused on the efficiency of individual workers, quickly spread to the office, and eventually encompassed the home environment as well. Taylor sought a one best way to do every job, standardizing work methods and tools in order to increase productivity. *Taylorism* , as it was called, began to change the way organizations functioned. Before this time, organizations were usually set up in homes or informal businesses where the workspaces were open. There were no barriers to communication and ideas could flow freely among employees. Instead, manufacturing areas and offices were separated, work became specialized, procedures became fixed and efficiency increased. Unfortunately communications decreased. Temporarily at least, human relations took a back seat to productivity. This was not Taylor's intention. He was trying to make it easier for the employees as well as have them increase productivity. Although he didn't coin the "work smarter, not harder" phrase, this was his intention.

Frank and Lillian Gilbreth also had an impact by introducing time and motion study to the manufacturing process. The Gilbreths had twelve children and the movie *Cheaper by the Dozen* was based on their lives. They demonstrated that the same principles being applied in business could be adapted to the home. Their work gave rise to industrial engineering, time studies, and incentive standards, and a continuous pursuit of efficiency, not only in the plants but in offices as well.

What this quest for efficiency did in most cases was alienate the workers. Human relationships took a back seat. People were in separate areas or offices, took timed coffee breaks and lunch hours at specific times, and in many cases punched a clock every time they came and went – to keep track of hours worked. Workers were disciplined for chatting too long at the water cooler or kidding around in the factory. Policies, procedures and rules were developed. They usually stifled employee interaction, discouraged creativity and generated greater union activity. So the backlash, if I can call it that, was the human relations movement, where it was felt that a happy worker was a productive worker. We went from isolated offices to cubicles without doors, landscaped offices with movable partitions or no partitions, office Supervision changed from an authoritative or dictator style to a consultative or participative style. But that era, and the organizational development era that followed were motivated by the same desire to maximize employee productivity. parties and Christmas bonuses. A lot of time clocks were eliminated. Communication meetings were introduced and so on. It's ironic that the current digital era that we're in now is once again dehumanizing the work environment, decreasing personal interaction, reducing our creativity, and in some ways putting us back into the scientific management era. But this time we are doing it *willingly* rather than having it imposed on us. And it's mainly because we're being seduced by technology.

# PART 1: PRODUCTIVITY

# THE CHANGING ENVIRONMENT

The business world has changed a lot in the past thirty years. I smile when I think of some of the suggestions I used to make in my time management seminars. We were still talking about using dictation equipment for business letters, installing car phones and answering machines and handling the reams of junk mail. We were urging people to use hand-written speedy memos, self-inking stamps and pocket recorders when traveling. Most managers had offices, access to secretaries, and opportunities to delegate work to others. Quiet hours, intercepted visitors and screened telephone calls were common strategies for concentrating on the task at hand.

Most time management experts were expounding the merits of "To Do" lists, time logs and multitasking. There were no Internet, laptops, PDAs, smartphones, email or voice activated software. Most people worked from 9 AM to 5 PM. We urged them to leave their briefcases at the office when they went home, get up earlier, stagger their lunch hours and prioritize their "to Do" lists.

Of course we also suggested things that are still just as valid today, such as setting goals, planning, scheduling their priorities and organizing their work environment. Over the years, managing stress and life balance were justifiably added as the speed and complexity of life increased.

But the environment, and in most cases, the jobs themselves, have changed. We are becoming a more mobile society and many people no longer work from offices but are either at home or on the road. One of my recent clients consisted of case managers who seldom visited a centralized office. They were all equipped with laptops and did their administrative work onsite at their client's place, in their cars or at home. Since 2006, laptops have outsold desktop computers and in 2008, more businesses purchased laptops than desktops. Now handheld electronic devices such as iPhones, BlackBerrys and iPads seem to be outselling everything.

The pace of life has increased. Stress has increased. The incidence of ADD and ADHD are increasing. We are experiencing health problems such as obesity, diabetes, cancer and other diseases at increasing rates. We are suffering memory loss and lack of focus. There is also a breakdown in the family unit.

Performance now depends more on self-control than external control. Idle time and free or discretionary time is disappearing. Skills essential to personal productivity – the executive skills – are under attack. Working hours are increasing, impacting life balance, sleep, and interpersonal relationships. Family time is decreasing and is shifting from interactive activities such as charades, cards & board games to computer & video games. Computers deceive us into thinking that multitasking increases efficiency. Interruptions have become the number one time problem; but are accepted as a way of life. Reflection time, renewal time and time for creativity all continue to decrease. New addictions are forming, including the need to connect to electronic media such as email, social media, the Internet and video games.

**Speed is the new currency**

In my opinion, personal productivity has changed very little in the past 30 years in spite of technology. The net result of technology has been to speed up the pace of life. We are working faster, driving faster, communicating faster, eating faster – in short, living faster. The time savings gained by technology have been offset by increases in complexity, choices, interruptions, expectations, stress, delays and errors. Our bodies are not designed to operate at warp speed and we are faced with a variety of ailments to the point that "getting well" has become another time consumer.

No generation has had such a long lifespan as this current generation, yet a third of Americans claim they do not have enough time. In some respects, all we have done by introducing technology and increasing speed is reduce the time we spend on trivial and low-priority activities so we can spend time on more trivial and low-priority activities.

For example, washing machines do a wash quicker than when my mother used a scrubbing board; but now we do more washing. We have more clothes to wash and we wash them more often. Email is faster than writing or typing letters but we send & receive more messages. We are driving faster but spending the same amount of time in the car. It is believed that traveling time has been constant since ancient times. We have faster vehicles but longer distances to travel, plus more traffic, more construction and more gridlock.

Life in general is being lived at a much faster pace than 50 years ago – or even 20 years ago. We have a love affair with speed. And it borders on the ridiculous. From fast food and instant downloads to one-minute bedtime stories and drive-through funerals, businesses are competing for our discretionary time.

The average business lunch is down to 36 minutes or less. One article claims the average worker eats lunch in 24 minutes. The expression "lunch hour" is a misnomer. Everyone seems intent on packing more and more into every hour, some even gobbling down fast food as they check their email.

**The hazards of speed**

In order to get everything done, we are sacrificing sleep

and discretionary time. The average person now gets 90 minutes less sleep a night than she did a century ago. Drowsiness causes more car accidents than alcohol. In my lifetime, the average amount of sleep we get has decreased from just over 8 hours per night to 6.7 hours. Getting less than 6 hours of sleep a night can impair motor coordination, speech, reflexes and judgment.

Because we don't make time to eat properly, exercise properly or sleep sufficiently, we are becoming obese. It is an epidemic in the U.S. Up to a third of Americans are clinically obese. It's interesting to note that children in schools within walking distance of fast food restaurants tend to be obese. About 20% of Canadians are obese. The situation seems to be better if we have to walk farther to get to our fast food restaurants.

If we are walking faster, talking faster, driving faster, working faster, sleeping less, and using technology, why isn't productivity going through the roof and what happened to all that extra leisure time?

I feel we are accomplishing little more than we have always accomplished. We're just doing it at a higher speed. The time saved is being filled by interruptions and low priority activities.Studies show on average, each person loses 28% of the workday due to interruptions and inefficiency. I have seen similar statistics, such as 2.1 hours per day lost in interruptions.

Technology has helped convince us that multitasking saves time when the opposite is true. Studies show that when we switch back and forth from one task to the next, our brains' neural circuits take a small break in between – a time consuming activity that could reduce our efficiency by 50%.

In this fast-paced environment, many traditional strategies

are losing their impact or simply no longer work. Quiet hours, as we know them, are a thing of the past. "To Do" lists are losing their effectiveness. Focus is becoming weak or non-existent. Multitasking has become counterproductive. In some cases, even goal-setting has become ineffective. Eating on the run has become the norm. Sleep, in many cases is seen as an annoying necessity. We are spending more time on getting well than on staying healthy. The division between work and personal life has become blurred. Discretionary time is disappearing. ADD, stress, inefficiency, and lack of balance are all commonly associated with our changing environment.

There are advantages offered by technology but there are also disadvantages Technology is eliminating the division between work and home. With PDAs and cell phones we can be contacted at any time. Our *To Do* list travels with us wherever we go. So we have to be self-disciplined enough to ignore email and turn off our cell phone

But regardless of whether we are on a flexible hour system, or we're a telecommuter or a frequent flyer, the line between work and personal time has become blurred. We can work in the evening, in a car or at a ball park. Work is no longer a place but a state of mind. The boundaries that once dictated how we spend our time have become blurred or non-existent. Instead of three distinct segments of time – work, home and leisure – we have ended up with one large space filled with a mixture of work, home and leisure. You should stop thinking about work as a place you go to spend 8 or 9 hours a day, but as something you *do*. And much of it could be done anywhere.

It is just as important to schedule time with family, time alone and leisure time as it is to schedule business meetings, appointments and other business activities. We should be continually asking ourselves if the total time we are spending with our family and loved ones is in line with how much we value them. Schedule your work around your life; don't schedule your life around your work. Otherwise work may spread throughout our entire day and crowd out our personal activities, putting our lives out of balance. Most people don't need help *knowing* their priorities; they need help *living* their priorities. And of course that involves using a planning calendar, which we will cover later.

# UNDERSTANDING TIME MANAGEMENT

Organizing is the act of rearranging *items* that are in a disorganized, cluttered state so that everything can be retrieved quickly with less effort, maximizing both their utility and visual appeal. Time management refers to increasing both the *efficiency and the effectiveness* of individuals and organizations through the organization of *tasks and events* by using tools such as planners and computers, and techniques and processes such as goal-setting, planning and scheduling. The two activities are interrelated since disorganization normally wastes time. The major difference between *organizing* and t*ime management* is that, in general, organizing deals with *things* and time management deals with *activities* that have a time dimension. Both are important.

**Time management continuum**

Time management and personal organization are on a continuum. That is, there are degrees of organization, ranging from completely disorganized and chaotic to complete freedom from being disorganized and at a stage where we are experiencing maximum effectiveness. Probably few of us ever experience complete freedom from disorganization, but that's what we aim for. Time management, including organization, is a process rather than an event. The diagram below illustrates how time management, including organization, is a process and not a single event. You should find this encouraging, because it's not a matter of being organized or disorganized or being a good time manager or a poor time manager. You could already be a third of the way there or two-thirds of the way there.

**Efficiency vs. effectiveness**

Productivity is a measure of output per unit of input - such as the number of widgets manufactured per hour or the number of units sold in a day. A person can be more productive if she gets things done in fewer hours. But we don't know the *value* of some of the things she gets done. Getting more things done in less time says nothing about the *quality* of those things. Efficiency is concerned with getting more things done in less time, thus increasing productivity. Effectiveness, on the other hand, assures you that you are getting the *right* things done. For example, developing life goals, plans, policies and mission statements are all aimed at increasing effectiveness. But reducing interruptions or improving e-mail and streamlining meetings are aimed at being more efficient. Similarly, personal values, career choices and life balance all aid effectiveness. Office organization, file management and the use of technology are aimed at increasing efficiency. Efficiency is doing something in the best possible way, while effectiveness is doing the best possible thing. Effectiveness may involve having a vision or mission, goals compatible with that vision, and a plan of action to achieve those goals or objectives. But efficiency is necessary to carry out the step-by-step action plan in the most economical, expedient way with a resultant quality consistent with the goal. A goal and plan are useless if the job never gets done. Efficiency cuts through procrastination, perfectionism and inertia, and converts a plan into action. Efficiency minimizes delays, interruptions, distractions and ensures that results are obtained. Efficiency and effectiveness work in tandem; one is useless without the other. Without effectiveness, we lack direction drift away from the priorities, and become busy without accomplishing the 20% of the tasks which represent 80% of the value. On the other hand, without efficiency we experience the frustration of knowing exactly where we want to go, but seeing little progress in that direction. It's a "two steps forward and one step backwards" process. Effectiveness has an eye to the future while efficiency deals with the here and now. A manager, who is effective, sets goals, plans, organizes, directs, controls and innovates. The one who is efficient conducts the "doing" portion of his or her job with a minimum of interruptions, idle time, procrastination, indecision, perfectionism or wasted effort. Efficiency looks at the process through a microscope, analyzing every detail of the jobs to eliminate, simplify, combine, or improve segments of them so the total process can be accomplished in a minimum of time at minimum cost with minimum effort. Effectiveness looks at a process through a wide-angle lens, observing how it affects the productivity of the other processes, how it contributes to the goals of the organization and how it impacts the bottom line. Efficiency studies may lead to an improvement in a process or job. Effectiveness studies may serve to eliminate it. Although both are important, effectiveness studies should come first, since there's little point in improving something that may later be eliminated. Never underestimate the importance of efficiency; but never strive for efficiency at the expense of effectiveness. The higher the level in the organization, the more time a manager must spend managing, and less time actually doing. Therefore, effectiveness becomes more essential at higher levels in the organization, while efficiency is critical at the staff level. But even a CEO has a certain amount of *doing* and limited time for its accomplishment. Efficiency never loses its importance. Although time management experts urge us not to be efficient at the expense of effectiveness, this should not be construed to mean efficiency is unimportant. Lacking effectiveness is like sailing a ship without a rudder. But it is no less serious to be sailing a rudder without a ship.

**Don't confuse busy work with real work**

Real work advances your business or job while busywork it is what you do to avoid real work. Real work includes things such as planning, goal setting, creative thinking, problem solving and decision-making. There is little visible activity with this type of work – consequently busywork looks more like real work that real work does. There is a tendency on the part of many people to keep busy, which has little if anything to do with being effective. We should judge others by their actual results, not by their physical activity. I would be suspicious of any businessperson who was constantly in motion. When communicating, if you're always talking, you can't be listening. Similarly, in business, if you're always busy working, you can't be doing much planning, goal setting, creative thinking or problem-solving. And these are essential activities that simply can't be multitasked. Doing things right the first time saves time in the long run. Rushing through jobs or multitasking while you do them is not a smart thing to do. It is even more important to do the right things. Spending time on unnecessary jobs is little better than sitting idle for the same period of time. In fact it could be worse; because if you were doing nothing, at least you would be relaxing. Being a 100% perfect at doing the wrong thing is still 100% waste of time. Think before you act. Is that task really necessary? Does it contribute to your goals? Does it further your career or contribute to your well-being? One of the keys to effective time management is to be selective in what you do. There simply isn't enough time to do everything. If there were time for all the things you *should* be doing there would be no problem. You could simply do everything and the priorities would all get done along with all the other stuff. The fact is, our time is limited. Doing everything is not an option. Doing one thing means *not* doing something else. And there is a big difference between the things that *should* be done and the things that *must* be done.

### Holistic time management

Internal Time Management, our mind's perception of time, is one aspect of the holistic time management approach, I gave a definition of holistic time management as I see it:

*The strategies necessary to lead a happier, healthier, longer, more productive & fulfilling life.* Longevity is more important than efficiency, even from the standpoint of traditional time management. Sure you can do things faster and better and save ten minutes here and ten minutes there and eventually may even gain the equivalent of two extra years of work accomplished in your lifetime. But wouldn't it make more sense to simply live two years longer? Even if you only maintained your current level of efficiency, you would not only get as much work done; you would also have two extra years to enjoy whatever life has to offer.

As soon as you bring longevity into the equation, good health becomes an important factor. And since you don't want your body to outlive your mind, you must also pay attention to your cognitive skills, and since you will want to maintain purpose and fulfillment throughout your lifetime, you need to include spirit. So holistic time management must involves everything that affects body, mind and spirit. Now it is truly holistic – and a lot broader area of study than the traditional time management that we are discussing in this book. If we are in top shape physically, mentally and spiritually, we know that we will be more productive – as well as have a much greater chance of extending our lifespan.

**Internal time management**

Although the focus in traditional time management training programs is on external time management or "clock" time, the greatest improvement in personal productivity is possible only through internal control. You can have an organized environment, clear goals and the top priorities scheduled in your planner or PDA and still fail to accomplish anything of significance. Weak "executive skills" such as initiating work, staying on task, controlling impulses, and regulating emotions can sabotage any time management strategy – whether it is planning, prioritizing or scheduling. But willpower, self-discipline, attentiveness, focus, and other internal time management strategies can be developed. Self-defeating behaviors such as procrastination and perfectionism can be reduced. And working *with* your biological clock instead of *against* it will make it easier to accomplish more with less effort. These are all important aspects of internal time management, which to date has been virtually ignored. Internal time management is just one of eight areas that you must explore if you wish to improve productivity through the new concept of holistic time management. It involves working in sync with your biological clock, and recognizing and capitalizing on the brain's role in how you both perceive and manage time. The other areas of holistic time management are health, organization, lifestyle, spirituality, traditional time management, interpersonal relationships, and cognitive skills, which I will explore in a future book.

**Early birds and night owls**

Larks, or "early birds" as they are sometimes called, are not often appreciated by the "night owls," Especially if they live in the same house. That's why I am tip-toeing around the condo in the early morning while my wife slumbers. For people in a similar situation it is wise to adjust schedules so each person can do their thing without disturbing the other people in the house. My early morning walk and exercise and "focus hour" at a local coffee shop, for instance, allows my wife to sleep undisturbed. And converting a den into a "reading room" allows my wife to read into the wee hours of the morning while I snore in isolation in the bedroom. It's important to recognize that everyone's biological clock is not the same. Larks are at a full head of steam by mid-morning and probably produce their most creative work before noon. But don't expect them to be fully awake for an evening meeting. And never expect them to be creative at that time. "Owls," on the other hand are usually most alert around 6 pm, and frequently do their best work in the evening. I t's not a case of being one or the other. Most people are in between a lark and an owl and you could be anywhere on the continuum. Only about ten percent of us are larks, twenty percent are night owls, and the rest are somewhere in between. There is a core period, somewhere in the middle of the day, where all groups are operating on all cylinders. So unless you know how everyone's biological clock is calibrated, it is probably best to schedule brainstorming sessions or arduous projects half way through the day. Oh, but avoid the "nap zone" somewhere around 3 PM. According to Medina, that's when the brain wants to take a nap, and doesn't really care what the owner is planning to get done at that time.

### Use prime time for priorities

Prime time is when you are at your peak energy level and more mentally alert and able to tackle difficult tasks. If you don't know the prime hours of your own biological clock, try a different task, such as a crossword puzzle, at different times during the day – when you first get up, at 10 AM, at noon, 2 PM, 4 PM, 6 PM, and 10 PM. Then decide when you found the puzzle easiest. Most people seem to have their prime time in the morning; but not necessarily when they first get up. And when time management experts tell you to get up an hour earlier and get a head start on the day, this may not be good advice. Getting up earlier could be counterproductive. It depends upon whether you are a *morning person* or a *night person* . And also what is meant by *earlier* . If it's before 6 AM, forget it, according to researchers. In general, that's the time we're least alert. Our ability to think clearly and react quickly is at its lowest point between 3 AM and 6 AM.

# PLANNING

In this digital age of speed with high-tech devices, both how we use them and the environment in which we use them are constantly changing. We can no longer have a "To Do" list mentality and still survive. Planning is more important than ever. Things change so rapidly, it seems as though the present is overlapping the future. You could use the analogy of driving to work through traffic. You don't know what the holdup is ahead; you only know that you have come to a standstill. And your focus is on inching forward one car length at a time. But if I were to lift you up in a helicopter so you could see for miles ahead, you would know that there is a major accident six blocks down the road, and that you could easily avoid it by making a right turn just ahead and traveling along a parallel street. Seeing the future that awaits you allows you to make adjustments in the present. Similarly, in business and in life in general, you must see beyond your daily "To Do" list and weekly schedules and get a glimpse of the future and how you can best adjust and prepare now for what lies ahead. I refer to this as "helicopter planning" – rising above the busyness of each day and spending a portion of your time visualizing and planning for the future. I use the analogy of a helicopter because it can rise straight up, getting some space between you and the current situation, and it can hover so you still have a good view of what's going on now, while still looking ahead to see what the situation will be further down the road if you continue doing what you are doing. All successful business owners need to get out of their day-to-day busyness and make time for long-range planning. So helicopter planning requires that you get some space between you and the clutter and busyness of everyday operations. It could be in the form of a weekend retreat with a few business advisors or in a local hotel for or a day or two in an unstructured meeting alone or with your advisory board, partners or whatever. If you are a one-person business, the least you should do is block off a half day each week or two – dedicated to business planning. This is the time that you're no longer working in the business, but on the business. Since Tuesday is considered to be the most productive day of the week, you might want to leave that time to work on the plan that you develop. You might consider a Friday morning, for your helicopter planning. Or you could make it Saturday morning if necessary. You might recruit two or three retired businesspeople to serve as an advisory board. There are probably more than enough people who would gladly volunteer their services. All successful business owners need to get out of their daily grind and find time for helicopter planning. If you are not in business, you can still use the same concept for your personal life. In this case you would involve your family as well. In these planning sessions you might focus on areas of the business that are critical to making it to next month, the next quarter and next year. You will have to decide which three or four priorities take precedence over everything else. These might be such things as managing cash flow, focusing on customers and quality service, and accelerating revenue growth. For personal planning, it might involve your career, financial status, self-development, family vacation, and so on. Since change is occurring so rapidly, long-range planning is shrinking in length. We used to think of long-range planning as being 10 or more years with medium-range being five or more and short-range being one year or more. Now you could consider five years long-range and short-range six months or less.

**The Sigmoid Curve**

Charles Handy in his book, *The Age of Paradox*, makes an interesting case for launching a second career *before* the first one starts going downhill. or a second business *before* the first one starts to falter or a new product before the sales on the first one starts to peter out. Handy feels the *Sigmoid Curve*, an s-shaped curve tilted forward, sums up the story of life. For example, if we start a new business, we usually start slowly, sales take off, and then level off and finally start to decrease. The time to make a change is while we're approaching the crest of the curve, while everything is going great. At that point we have the energy and resources needed to get a new curve through its faltering first stage. But we are reluctant to change when things are going great and tend to ride the first curve down to oblivion. The various stages of growth are marked on the diagram. Take products for example. I have developed well over 50 products over the last 30 years, if you include manuals, self-study programs, books, training programs, videos and so on. But we probably had less than 30 available on our website at any one time. You can't wait until one product fizzles out before developing a new product. When things are going well, it's easy to sit back and do nothing. My public seminars were still doing well when I started doing teleseminars, and electronic products on flash memory sticks were developed long before book sales declined. You shouldn't wait for sales to plummet before introducing something new. You can guess the fate of paper planners. Although I think the Taylor Planner is a more effective planning tool than any electronic handheld device, I didn't have to wait until we were bankrupt to see that paper planner sales would no longer support our business. My experience in large companies showed that such things as austerity programs and cost-cutting measures took place whenever the company was on a downswing – at a time when the company could ill afford the damaged morale and resentment that normally ensued. By then it was too late anyway. Band-Aid approaches seldom work. Companies should have examined their spending habits during prosperous times when sales and profits were soaring. Living high on the hog during good times and panicking during recession is no way to run a company. A similar situation could occur in our personal life as well. If we get a higher paying job, an inheritance, a big sale or some other sudden influx of money, we might go on a spending spree that eventually escalates to a lifestyle. And when the source of the extra money dries up, we find ourselves unable to stop the downward spiral to personal bankruptcy. It's difficult to determine where we are on the sigmoid curve at any point in time, only that we're on an upswing or a downswing. But companies usually underestimate how far they are on the upswing. Taking action before reaching the peak is a lot better than finding we're on the verge of a downward slide. Successful companies introduce new products; packaging or other innovations while things are going well, not as attempts to turn things around. The things that make you successful are rarely the things that keep you there. The environment in which we live keeps changing. It takes courage and a degree of risk to change things when everything's going well. But if you don't, it may lead to disaster.

The *Sigmoid Curve* because it is more than just planning, it's anticipation.

How do you know where you are on the curve? You don't really know until it's too late. So you must guess. In this fast-paced environment where change is exponential, it's likely that you're farther along on the curve than you think. In his book, *The Age of Paradox*, Charles Hardy refers to a study of

208 companies over a period of 18 years to find out which ones were consistently successful. Only three companies lasted for the entire 18 years. 52 percent could not maintain their record for more than 2 years. By that example, it would be reasonable to introduce change after 2 or 3 years. If you start a second curve too soon there are no great consequences. Start too late and it could mean disaster. But Handy's book was published back in 1994. Since then we have entered the digital age of speed, and everything has accelerated, I suggest that we develop new products, services, strategies, innovations or whatever every 6 months, not every 2 years. Just look at today's newspapers and note how quickly companies such as RIM and Microsoft and Apple are launching new products or upgrades. What used to be long-range planning is now short-range planning, and short-range planning has become immediate. The things that don't change rapidly include our vision of what we want to do and become in the future, our mission statement, and our personal policies. They are all included in the planning process.

**Vision**

Your vision is simply what you visualize yourself doing in the future, say 10, 15 or more years from now. If time, money and circumstances were not factors, how would you spend the rest of your life? What turns you on? What did you enjoy doing as a child? What are you good at doing? What do other people say you are good at doing? This requires time for reflection. Think about what you were doing in the past when you lost all awareness of time and were completely absorbed by the activity - so much so that you didn't want it to end. What do you dream and fantasize about? No hurry. This is an ongoing self-analysis that could take weeks, months or even years. Once you discover what you want to do for the rest of your life – your passion or purpose for living – it becomes your motivator. It gives you a reason to get up every morning and to persist through hardships and set-backs to do what you were created to do. When you are fulfilling your purpose in life you are self-actualizing.

**Mission statement**

Once you decide what it is you are going to do, who you will do it for or to, how you will do it and the purpose for doing it, you express this in the form of a mission statement. I have virtually the same mission statement today and it has kept me from being side-tracked from what I do best. Each year I enter my mission statement in the space provided near the front of my *Taylor Planner* . Currently it reads as follows:

*To help individuals and organizations manage their time and their lives, through time management training, products and services, so they are able to free up time to work on their personal and organizational goals.*

Mission statements should be brief – one sentence if possible – so it can easily be reduced to writing and committed to memory. If it's a company or organization, every staff member should understand it. It provides direction and focus in your business. It should be clear, brief and memorable. If it's a personal mission statement it should reflect who you are. Goals are specific. They tell you exactly what you will do, when you will do it and how you will do it. But a mission statement explains *why* you will do it. I encourage people to have a personal mission statement that reflects what they want to do with their life. My personal mission statement is essentially the same one that I use for my company because it is my passion. I truly believe it is my life purpose and I continue to do it long past the age of retirement – whether I get paid for it or not.

**Personal policies**

Corporate policies such as *the customer is always right, we will not be undersold* and *satisfaction or money refunded* have been around for over a century. They serve as guidelines for employees to make tough decisions, provide consistency and express the organization's philosophy. They also save time. It is similarly effective for *individuals* to develop a set of *personal* policies or value statements to help guide them through life. Policies help people make decisions regarding their personal use of time and prevent them from getting involved in activities inconsistent with their beliefs. I also wrote down, some personal policies, such as I *will not accept speaking engagements on Sundays,* and *I will work only two evenings per month.* I didn't want to accept a lot of evening work since I would soon find myself speaking every night of the week telling people to manage their time and spend more time with their families. You have to walk your talk. So it makes sense to draw up some personally policies to guide you through life.

Here are some examples of personal policies.
I will not compromise my beliefs, values or personal mission.

- I will not attempt to do two things in the same time frame or be all things to all people.

- At no time will other peoples' lack planning become my crisis.

- I will not become an activity packrat; for every new activity I take on, one of equal time value will be subtracted.

- I will have as much respect for my own time as I have

for other peoples' time.

- Business decisions or choices affecting my family will be discussed in advance with my family.

- I will not be coerced into changing my priorities; they will be changed only if my heart is in it.

- At no time will I take on projects that conflict with my personal values.

*A policy is a predetermined course of action that guides and determines present and future decisions.*

Personal policies will save us time and frustration by speeding up the decision-making process. Personal policies could also include such statements as *I will always get up at 6 AM, I will not work on weekends*, or *I will save 10 percent of my pay*.

Personal policies help us develop self-discipline in areas where we tend to be weak. A policy of *never eating between meals*, for example, once we adhere to it for a few weeks, becomes a habit. Eventually, it will take little willpower to say no to an afternoon snack since we say it automatically.

Personal policies also help us to achieve goals, since they are *standing plans* that lead us in a specific direction, such as towards financial independence, cardiovascular fitness, weight loss, etc. They provide stability in our lives and accountability for us. To establish personal policies you must first determine the values you want to protect and the image you want to project. Once you are clear on your priorities and how you want to use your time, put your statements in writing and post them where they'll be a constant reminder. This might be at the front of your planner or in your PDA or other electronic organizer. Be sure to discuss your policies with family members or others who will be affected by them. You could end up modifying them, but be sure that you end up with a set of guidelines that reflect *your* beliefs, not those of others. With your personal policies in place, you will be able to say *no* at the appropriate times, and use your discretionary time wisely. For example, if someone asks you to serve on a volunteer committee, your policy prompts you to say *no* unless you can free up time for it by releasing a current activity. You won't have to waste time deliberating or taking it under consideration or giving the person false hope with a *maybe* . Or if you were asked to do something unethical, you would quickly refuse. Policies speed up the decision-making process and prevent you from straying from your life mission. Policies are guidelines, not rules. They are flexible depending on the situation. For instance, you may decide not to refuse to work overtime if your job actually depended on it. However, if you were consistently confronted with overtime at the threat of losing your job, you would either start looking for another job or change your policy. You cannot continue to live in opposition to your personal values. To do so would increase stress, diminish your self-esteem and take much of the fun out of life. Your policies can be modified as time passes. Your priorities may change as your situation changes. As people grow older, for instance, they may have a greater respect for free time and less respect for money. Single people may have different priorities if they marry and have children. The important thing is that we maintain control of our lives by deciding our priorities and how we spend our time. Policies help us to live by design, not by default. I usually ask people to try writing out some personal policy statements that will help achieve goals that they have set for themselves. It's good to review them each morning until they are committed to memory. Then adhere to them throughout the days ahead.

# SHAPING YOUR FUTURE WITH GOALS

Goals-setting is instrumental to the effective use of your time. Without goals, you will not know what's important and what you should schedule in your planner. It's important to set goals in all areas of your life, including business or career, self-development, family, health and spiritual goals. Everyone knows they should be working on priorities. But many of us struggle with identifying the priorities. It sometimes seems like everything's important. By setting goals, you will are identifying the top priorities in your life.

I find in my workshops that most people do not have clear cut goals in writing. Many don't believe they need goals. After all, they have a good job, a happy home life, and are enjoying their current lifestyle. Why bother with goals? I have developed a brief exercise that you can use to determine whether goals would help you in enjoying life to the fullest. If you don't need goals, fine. But in my experience, most people who claim they don't need goals end up playing the "If only" game later in life – "If only I had done this and if only I had done that." If you are not convinced that having specific personal goals in writing would make any difference, you could use the following exercise, which I refer to as the *Extrapolation Technique*.

**The extrapolation technique**
Draw two vertical lines on a sheet of paper to form three columns as illustrated in the form example that follows. In the left hand column, enter all the areas in your life that are important to you, such as your job or profession, education, income, major accomplishments, health family, travel, etc., and jot down your present status in each of these areas. In the second column, indicate where you'll be in each of these ar-

eas in ten years, assuming you keep doing what you are doing now. In other words, extrapolate your life. You may be thinking about attending night courses, buying a house, changing jobs, going on a diet, or any number of things. But if you are not actually doing anything about it at this time, chances are that's what you'll be doing about it in ten years – nothing. There's a big difference between intention and commitment. When you work on this exercise, be honest with yourself. If you have not registered for that education program yet or have not started saving for that new house or have not blocked off time for your family this week, what makes you think that you will do so in the immediate future? It's so easy to procrastinate. Of course, you may *not want* to make any changes to your current lifestyle. Perhaps where you will be in ten years is exactly where you *want* to be – doing the same things you're doing now. If that's the case, you don't need goals. But at least you can verify it with this exercise. This extrapolation exercise forces you to look at your future as well as your current situation. Continuing to do what you are doing will get more of what you are already getting, but little else. If you are not happy with where you will be in ten years, now is the time to do something about it. Fill in the third column with the things you would like to do, achieve, acquire and experience. These will become the basis for the goals that you will set for yourself. Then you only need to express them clearly and succinctly according to guidelines that we will provide you, record them in your planner, and schedule time to work on them.

### The Extrapolation Technique

| Current life Situa- | Extrapolating | Where I |

| tion | current lifestyle | would like to be in |
|---|---|---|
| 10 years | 10 years | |
| Date: | | |
| My Age: | | |
| Age of my family members (parents, spouse, children): | | |

Profession or occupation and brief summary of responsibilities:

Formal education completed and self-development courses taken:

Hobbies, leisure activities:

Annual Income:

Most important personal possessions:

| Current life Situation | Extrapolating current lifestyle | Where I would like to be in |
|---|---|---|
| | 10 years | 10 years |
| Total cash in the | | |

| | | |
|---|---|---|
| bank | | |
| Total money owed (mortgage, loans, credit cards etc.) | | |
| Investments, pension, life insurance, disability insurance, will: | | |
| Accomplishments that gave greatest sense of achievement, including travel: | | |

Associations in which I am actively involved:

Close friends and relatives I spend time with:

State of my health, weight, eating habits, exercise:

Spiritual growth and other significant areas of my life:

**What makes for effective goals?**

When providing information on goal setting, or anything else for that matter, it helps to use acronyms to make it easier for them to recall the information later. You have probably all heard of the acronym SMART for the requirements of effective goal setting.

**S**pecific (Exactly what you will do)
**M**easurable (So you know when you have reached it)
**A**ttainable (Realistic as opposed to pie in the sky dreams)
**R**esults-oriented (Describes what you are actually going to accomplish)
**T**ime-framed (deadline date on each goal)

There are a few other important characteristics of effective goal-setting that I suggest be represented by adding the word WAYS to the word SMART to make sure the information is complete. The WAYS stands for

**W**ritten (Preferably in your planner)
**A**ll areas of your life (To maintain balance)
**Y**our goals (Not other people's idea of what you should do)
**S**cheduled (Increases your chances of actually achieving the goals).

### Benefits of goal setting

- Creates a climate for motivation.

- Enables us to plan and gain greater control over our own destinies.

- Adds challenge to our lives and a sense of achievement.

- Provides a means of self-evaluation.

- Makes us results-oriented so we work smarter, not harder.

- Adds a new dimension of meaning to our lives.

- Enables us to manage our time more effectively.

- Reduces the stress normally attributed to the feeling of "not getting anywhere".

- Increases our chances of success.

- Allows us to determine whether our jobs are compatible with the things we really want out of life.

It's one thing to have goals, but quite another matter to achieve them. That's why scheduling time to work on them is so important. "To Do" lists are intentions; but scheduled appointments with yourself to work on your goals and other priorities are the real commitments.

# CONVERTING PLANS INTO ACHIEVEMENTS

Scheduling is the first step in converting plans to achievements. Time should be scheduled to work on your goals. An ideal planner shows a week at a glance with sufficient space to jot down the name of the project or the task you will be working on. It should include all seven days as well as evenings. The *priority* items from your To Do list are spread throughout the week so you can actually see at a glance how much of your time is being consumed. It would be foolish to take on more commitments this week if all you time is already spoken for – unless you are willing to displace one of those priority tasks that you have already scheduled. The point is that a To Do list and a pocket calendar just won't do. You have a lot of choices in planners but it needs to have more than little squares for the days. You need to be able to spread your activities throughout the days and weeks and there should be space enough to schedule the more important items directly into time slots. We all have more things to do than we can possibly get done. But we can insure the important ones get done by blocking off time in our planner to get them done. A To Do list is only an intention. A scheduled block of time is a commitment. A planner should be used for scheduling appointments with *yourself*, not just appointments and meetings with others. "To Do" lists encourage procrastination if not used correctly and in moderation. The trouble with many people is that they lack focus. A small business owner, for instance, may haphazardly do everything she can to increase profits rather than focus on the 20 percent of the possible actions that would lead to 80 percent of the results. A planner allows you to focus on what's important by scheduling goal-related activities directly into its pages. So if you feel it's imperative to write a book in order to gain credibility as a consultant, you would estimate how much time it would take to write a book. Initially it's a wild guess. After working on the project for a few weeks you can adjust the time allowance. If you estimate 100 hours of uninterrupted work to complete a project and you have 50 weeks to complete it, you would have to schedule 2 hours of uninterrupted time each week to complete the project. But there's no such thing as uninterrupted work, so you schedule 3 hours per week to allow for those unexpected interruptions or self-interruptions that are bound to occur. It varies depending on the nature of your job, but as a rule of thumb, I schedule about 50% more time than I think the job will take.

If you find it difficult to block off a 3-hour chunk of time in one day you might consider scheduling one and one half hours twice per week. There's a difference between what *should* be done and what *must* be done. Keep the *"shoulds"* on a *To Do* list but move the *" musts"* to specific time slots in your planner. To Do lists are one-dimensional – they tell you what has to be done; but they don't tell you how long those things will take or when you are going to do them. People usually put themselves on a To Do list and others in their schedule. So we end up meeting with all those people; but never get to our own priorities. The 80–20 rule applies to *To Do* lists as well. 80% of the items collectively contribute only 20% of the results. If you're in doubt about whether something should be scheduled or put on a *To Do* list, ask yourself, "What would be the consequences of not getting this done?" If the answer is "Very little," add it to your *To Do* list. The Pareto Principle or 80/20 rule tells us that the significant items in a given group normally constitute a relatively small portion of the total items in the group. I have always believed that it's best to record your *To Do* list, in your *planner,* not on separate sheets of paper. People are forever misplacing lists. And they often spend time copying the remaining items to another list. Your planner, on the other hand, is more difficult to misplace; it is with you everywhere you go, and the crossed off items are still visible so you can see what you have done in weeks gone by. With a weekly *To Do* list you have the option of spreading your things to do over several weeks. Each time a new task surfaces, you decide whether it should be done this week, next week or even later, and add it to that page. This makes your workload manageable. Whether you use a week at a glance or a day at a glance planner is a matter of personal preference. I prefer to see how my week is shaping up. I like to be able to instantly spot my plans for the entire week and see what time I have left for additional projects. A page of my planner is shown below. It has been reduced in size slightly, but you can get an idea of what it looks like. In the age of speed it is even more important to schedule your personal and family activities into the same planner in order to keep your life in balance. When you schedule time for tasks, always schedule more time that you think you need – because you will have interruption and must allow for them. Also don't schedule too tightly. I schedule about 25 to 30% of my planner in advance so there will be room to work on those other urgent priorities that always seem to crop up. For work activities, I don't schedule more than two weeks into the future. Otherwise I would be making too many changes.

### Choosing a planner

Planning involves visualizing the future you *want* and then taking the necessary action in the present in order to make that vision a reality. *Your goals are simply snapshots of the future you visualize.* These snapshots are then expressed in writing and entered into your planner as a constant reminder of where you are headed. Here are five things an effective planning calendar should include.

1. A place to record your goals since they are an integral part of the planning process.

2. A place to record your mission statement as well since it reminds you of why you your purpose in life and forms the launching pad for your goals

3. Each day broken into 15 minute increments, including Saturdays and Sundays as well as evenings to facilitate the scheduling of personal as well as business projects and activities.

4. Daily follow-up sections to record deadlines for assignments due, birthdays and other special events, and notes reminding you when to check the follow-up file.

5. Weekly and daily "To Do" sections to record non-priority items that should be done.

**Time for a "work break.**

Accept the fact that the business environment has lost much of its structure, and in many cases the people within that environment have lost their self-discipline. With the Internet, e-mail, and devices such as the iPad, iPhone and technology in general vying for our attention, our time is under attack 24/7. Interruptions, distractions and incessant communications are now the norm. We need strategies that allow us to cope in this digital age of speed, multitasking and constant interruptions. In the past we were able to successfully schedule coffee breaks to relax and unwind. I propose that we now schedule "work breaks" to get the important things done. Make these breaks relatively free from interruptions by engaging voice mail, turning off your smart phone, ignoring email and either closing your door or moving to a more isolated area such as a boardroom, vacant office or coffee shop. When scheduling "work breaks," do so in 90-minute chunks of time. Ninety minutes is a reasonable length of time to be unavailable to other people. It also minimizes self-interruptions & fatigue, allows you to capitalize on your "prime time" each day, avoids the inefficiency of marathon work sessions, and makes it easier to build a consistent habit of working productively each day. Those who think they are good at multitasking are usually the worst at it. Although researchers have identified a few "supertaskers," who can focus fully on two or more things at the same time, chances are we're not one of them. Stick to one task for 90 minutes – less if you find you can't focus that long. If you are able to get two of these work sessions into each day, you will be head and shoulders above most people when it comes to personal productivity.

**The 90-minute rule of scheduling**

Scheduled "work breaks" won't be entirely free of interruptions. You might even interrupt yourself as your mind wanders. Occasionally there will be real emergencies that you can't ignore. So when I schedule. 90 minutes, I do so with the belief that I will get at least one hour of productive work accomplished. Also, I find it's better to schedule time rather than tasks. It's so difficult to estimate how long it will take to complete a task or project, I find it is less frustrating and less stressful if you schedule one or two 90 minute periods each week to work on the project with the intention of completing it within the estimated timeframe to neutralize the Parkinson's Law effect, but without the pressure of a "do or die" deadline. This is one of the subtle changes to alleviate the stress that's inherent in today's workplace – but it's really just a shift in mindset. There are other reasons that I feel 90 minutes is a good choice. One of the biggest problems for most people is sustained attention, which is one of the "executive skills." Working for shorter periods of time is generally more efficient since the longer you work on a project, the more difficult it is to maintain focus, and the more susceptible you are to interruptions – either by yourself or others. Concentration rises and falls in 90 minute cycles, and I find that 90 minutes is about the maximum time that most people can concentrate without actually *looking* for interruptions. Many people can concentrate effectively for only 20 minutes or less. 90 minutes is an acceptable wait time for most people before they receive an answer to their e-mail, text message or phone call. Of course a few people expect instant replies, but those people are simply being unrealistic. 90 minutes isn't an unrealistic period of time to be unavailable to staff members either. 90-minute segments allow at least four major projects to be worked on each day – two in the morning and two in the afternoon – keeping the goal-related priorities on target. 90 minutes also allows prime time for at least two projects. This is usually in the mornings when most people experience their peak energy level and are most mentally alert. They also fit the typical day's schedule – two projects in the morning, and two in the afternoon, falling in line with the "time policy" concept described in my book, *Making Time Work for You.* 90 minutes is about the minimum length of "working time" before "make-ready" time becomes a factor and starts having a negative impact on your efficiency. If you select too brief a period of time, you spend as much time getting your materials and your mind ready as you spend working on the project. I recommend you actually schedule 90-minute "appointments with yourself" in ink if you use a paper planner since you have every intention of keeping those appointments. When we *react* to something, a different part of the brain is being activated than if we *plan* to do something. Writing down what we intend to do switches us to a more rational mode of thinking. When an interruption does occur, either something you think of or a remark someone else makes, jot it down so you can deal with it later. But continue with your planned activity. If you want to keep to do lists fine. But they should not replace "work breaks" People who work from To Do lists, without scheduling time in their planners to work on priorities, are seldom as effective as they could be in their jobs. Most people still work from To Do lists and only use their planner for scheduling meetings, appointments and major events. In my opinion this is the main reason for their lack of personal productivity, and excessive busyness and stress. Handheld electronic devices, if they are used as substitutes for paper planners, encourage the "To Do" list approach even more.

**Ten ways "To Do" lists can work against you.**

*To Do lists are intentions, not commitments*. Writing things down on the list only ensures that you won't forget them; but it doesn't mean you will do them. Making an appointment with yourself is more of a commitment. You have reserved the time in which To Do them. People could have a list of things To Do today and they could be in a meeting or seminar all day.

*To Do lists are only one dimensional*. They remind you of all the things you want To Do, but don't tell you how long they're going to take or when you are going To actually Do them. Scheduled activities, on the other hand, are three-dimensional and provide a more realistic indication of when they will be completed.

***To Do lists are open-ended.*** They don't give you any sense of closure or accomplishment since the list is never completed. Items are always being added. The tendency is to cross off as many items as possible – encouraging you to go for quantity of items as opposed to the important items.

***To Do lists are present oriented as opposed to future oriented*** . They keep you focused on the immediate things that have to be done as supposed to scheduled tasks, which force you to look at future days and weeks. By scheduling in the future you can see how the various tasks will affect the time you have available for other projects, activities and events.

***To Do lists are difficult to prioritize*** . It is impossible to list things in order of priority since you are always adding more things. People have tried rating them as A, B or C or highlighting the most important ones. Doing so still doesn't guarantee they will be done in that order. By scheduling, on the other hand, you are automatically prioritizing when you schedule something this week as opposed to next week, for instance. You are giving it priority treatment. And only important items should be scheduled anyway. So scheduling involves a selection process.

***To Do lists can be both stressful and overwhelming.*** To Do lists are never ending. It is depressing and de-motivational to have tasks that are never finished. The brain seeks closure, but that is impossible with a To Do list.

***To Do lists encourage overtime.*** Because of the brain's search for closure, the tendency is to complete everything on our To Do list, which of course is impossible. Daily To Do lists are even worse than weekly To Do lists. One study, conducted many years ago among pastors revealed that those who used daily To Do lists work longer hours than those who used weekly To Do lists. That's the reason we originally designed our planner with only a weekly To Do list.

***To Do lists separate the jobs you have to do from the time in which you will have To Do them.*** In fact many people keep separate To Do lists on pads or forms – separated altogether from their planners. If your planner does not include time for the priorities on your To Do list, that time will frequently be filled by other people's priorities. Items that are scheduled usually get done while items on a To Do list are usually postponed or abandoned.

***To Do lists are like buffets as opposed to planned dinners.*** With buffets it is easy to take on too much, choose the tasty items instead of the healthy ones, and waste time making choices. Planned the dinners require no decision. You get to eat what you have in front of you. And the planning allows those items to be the best ones for you – the priorities, so to speak.

***To Do lists are open invitations to natural tendencies that are counterproductive*** . For instance, we tend to work on those items that are easy, brief, pleasant and urgent, as well as those that please other people, rather than those that will further our own personal goals.

Now I have to say that To Do lists are better than trying to remember all the things you have To Do. At least, it gets your intentions into writing. You can always put everything on a To Do list and then select the most important ones to schedule. But To Do lists by themselves give you a false sense of accomplishment because people tend to measure progress by the number of items crossed off as opposed to the importance of the tasks completed. A recent survey by *Linkedin* found that only 11% of professionals actually complete all the tasks on their daily To Do lists. (Globe and Mail, June 15, 2012.)

**PDAs vs. paper planners**

Hand-held electronic computers can boost productivity immensely. But they are computers, not planners. Don't throw away the kitchen sink just because you buy a dishwasher. With a hard copy planner you can see your entire week, complete with scheduled tasks and your "things To Do" list at a single glance. Flipping a page brings you a whole new week of plans, appointments and projects. You can see your activities take shape, be completed and remain visibly intact as permanent trophies to your weekly accomplishments. A hardcopy planner also serves as a journal, reflecting not only your past activities, but your uniqueness – taking on your personality, character, and philosophy. It reveals your habits and style as well as your priorities. Color coding, sticky notes, self-adhesive labels and hand written notes can form a permanent footprint of your presence in this world and the impact you made. Nobody wants to be left behind in this information age where technology is king; but it's not a case of either using an electronic handheld device or using a paper planner. They both have their place. You can continue to plan and schedule using a paper planner while using your handheld device for contact information, databases, electronic communications, Internet access, and the dozens of other functions used on a regular basis such as GPS, photography, ebooks, email, banking and Google searches.

# MANAGING TECHNOLOGY

Leaders of the future will be those who can master some of the more useful technology that becomes available while maintaining their interpersonal skills. Not only will they be able to work efficiently, they'll be able to relate to other people, negotiate, gain consensus, close deals, network effectively and motivate and inspire others. Technology is good; but you can have too much of a good thing. Research published in the February, 2008 *Personality & Social Psychology Bulletin* , shows that daily social contacts may boost brain power and cognitive abilities. In a *University of Michigan* study of 3500 people, it was revealed that more time spent chatting with friends was associated with higher scores on memory tests. Interaction with people provides greater brain stimulation than watching a computer monitor or TV set. Technology, on the other hand, encourages multitasking, which in turn leads to stress, anxiety and inefficiency. Technology writer Danny O'Brien interviewed top achievers and found one thing in common that may account for their increased productivity. They all used some sort low-tech tool, such as a written "To Do" list or a plain paper pad. It pays to limit technology and maintain balance in your life. A UCLA study found that people who adopted a healthy lifestyle instead of constantly manipulating their BlackBerrys and cell phones showed improvement in memory scores and reasoning within a matter of weeks. Technology allows us to get trivial, unimportant tasks done faster so we can take on more trivial, unimportant tasks. We must be careful that technology doesn't become all-consuming and addictive. For many people it is already invading their personal space. An article in the November 12, 2012 Toronto Star reported on a survey by Infosecurity Europe in London that found that 70% of the workers surveyed spent at least a half hour a day working in bed. Another survey by Good Technology revealed that half of the office workers polled were answering emails while in bed. The trend is encouraged by suppliers who are offering everything from pyramid pillows to laptop trays designed specifically for bed workers. People in general are overloaded, stressed and ineffective because they have gotten away from the basic time management process of planning, setting goals, scheduling and getting the work done. They have bought into the "technology is everything" myth, and are so busy doing things, that they have no time to think or plan. As a result, much of what they are doing may be things of little importance, and they may be ignoring many of the things that are the most meaningful. By using technology indiscriminately, they are putting their lives in high gear, multitasking, responding to crises, and filling their lives with incessant interruptions and trivia. We are seduced into buying the latest gadget, and considered to be behind the times if we still use a land line or a paper planner. TV, itself addictive, glorifies video games, and by 2006, approximately 145 million people were playing video or computer games. According to Dr. Gary Small and Gigi Vorgan, in their book *iBrain,* players of one game spent an average of 22 hours per week at it. The average young person's brain is exposed to 8 hours of technology each day. Technology is becoming an addiction. You know something must be wrong when companies design 12-step programs to tackle email addiction. Or when psychiatric investigators in South Korea find that 20% of Internet-addicted children and teens end up with relatively severe ADHD symptoms. Or when people report a loss of energy and a sense of depletion after a marathon session with their TV or computer. People may believe they are in complete control of their lives, when the opposite is true. They are being *controlled* by technology. You can't say you are in control when you sleep with your BlackBerry, check email during a game of golf or spend 30 hours per week surfing the Internet.

Dr. Edward Hallowell, a psychiatrist in Sudbury, Massachusetts, and author of *Driven to Distraction*, sees a lot of patients wrapped up in this multitasking mania. Over the past decade he has seen a tenfold increase in the number of patients showing up with symptoms that closely resemble ADD, but of the work-induced variety. They were irritable, their productivity was declining, they couldn't get organized, they were making quick off-the-cuff decisions – all because they felt pressured to get things done quickly.

He gave the condition a name – *Attention Deficit Trait* (ADT) ( *Time Magazine* , January 10, 2006) ADT takes hold when we are unable to prioritize. They're not only distracted and impulsive, but feel guilty and inadequate. They feel it's their fault that they're falling behind. They think they have to work faster and longer, which only makes it worse. Technology, like most things, is good in moderation. But we seem to have forgotten that when you go high-tech, you also need more high-touch. Twitter and LinkedIn and text messaging and blogging are not the same as interacting one-on-one with people. People are good for your brain; technology, not so good. Research indicates that time spent chatting with friends in person tends to raise scores on memory tests. High-tech gadgets, video games, TV and the like have the opposite effect. In fact they have been shown to contribute to ADD in both adults and children. Chronic Internet and high-tech users tend to have poorer social skills and less focus. We should think twice before allowing time with email and the

Internet to crowd out time with family and friends. Top achievers combine high-tech with high touch. They interact socially, participate in face-to-face meetings, and even use paper-based systems such as planners or simple note pads as tools to get things done. I will never apologize for scheduling in a paper planner or drawing mind maps on a scratch pad or scribbling an idea on an index card. In fact people who think a BlackBerry or any kind of smart phone is a planner is mistaken.

### Why isn't productivity increasing?

In spite of technology, extended working hours and 24/7 connectivity, productivity in most countries is still falling. And yet, according to a recent article in the *Toronto Star* (Why Canada's productivity keeps falling, June 14, 2012), as our workforce shrinks, we must become more productive in order to sustain our high standard of living. I believe that major factor is the decreasing personal productivity of the workers. For example, the May 23, 2012 issue of the *Globe and Mail* reported on a survey of 65,000 people over the past decade that revealed the number one complaint was being distracted by the speech level while working at office cubicles. Not only is distraction increasing, we are becoming more vulnerable to distraction as our brains are being bombarded by digital technology. We are losing control. We are becoming more reactive than proactive and becoming slaves to technology. Worse still, we are accepting distraction as the norm and forming habits that keep us on a treadmill – working faster and longer but reaching fewer of our personal goals.

### Technology is a double-edged sword

Back in 2006, a survey by salary.com and AOL revealed

that employees, on average, spend 1.86 hours out of an 8-hour day doing something other than their jobs. And this does not include lunch and scheduled breaks. More than half the people surveyed said their biggest distraction during work hours is surfing the Internet for personal use. Other distractions included socializing, running errands outside the office, and simply "spacing out." According to *Inc. Magazine*, the cost to the companies of the time wasted in the 2006 survey was $544 billion. A year earlier a similar study showed that workers wasted just over 2 hours per day. But at that time, a third of the workers said they did so because they didn't have enough work to do, and others said they did so because they felt underpaid. I don't think too many people today would say they didn't have enough work to do. I'm not sure about the underpaid part. The sad thing is, the Internet and probably most technology, are time wasters as well as productivity boosters. Companies are not getting the full value out of technology.

**Don't get lost in the electronic jungle**
A 2011 poll conducted by Poll Position determined how many hours a day people spend looking at either TV, computer screen, e-reader, PDA or cellphone. About a third spend one to three hours, another third spend four to six, and the remaining third spend between seven and more than 10 hours a day viewing content on electronic devices. Much of this time was spent on social media and email. As of September 2012, there were eighty million BlackBerry subscribers worldwide. Social networking is now the most popular online activity, ahead of email, and accounts for almost 20 percent of the total time spent online. Facebook, for example, wasn't launched until 2004, and already has over one billion users. Europe tops the list, followed by Asia and then North Amer-

ica.

And the impact on time is obvious. The question we must ask ourselves is whether the time we are spending on electronic devices and social networking is helping us better achieve our personal goals or distracting us from them. So we must be purposeful, selective and self-disciplined when we navigate the electronic jungle.

### Is the Internet making us stupid?

We tend to ridicule those who print articles from the web instead of reading them in electronic format where they may be accompanied by links to supporting information, images and videos.When we go online, we enter an environment that promotes cursory reading, hurried and distracted thinking, and superficial learning. Links are particularly distracting, and studies show that jumping between digital documents impedes understanding. Comprehension declines whether or not people actually click on them. The depth of our intelligence hinges on our ability to transfer information from working memory (short-term memory) to long-term memory. But a bottleneck is created since working memory can only hold a relatively small amount at a time. When we are swamped with information, links, images, and advertising, the information spills over, so to speak, and doesn't make it into our long-term storage. It's like watering a house plant by continuing to pour on more water without giving it a chance to soak in. But when we read books for instance, we transfer information a little at a time into long-term memory and form associations essential to the creation of knowledge and wisdom.

# EMAIL

The habit that employees have of checking e-mail in the mornings, evenings and weekends has not gone unnoticed by employers. Many of them are more lenient on lateness as a result. But the scales tip in favor of the employers since 80% of those managers interviewed feel they could call employees at home at night. Mozy Inc., a U.S. – based company surveyed 500 employers and 500 employees in France, Germany, Ireland, UK and the USA. The bottom line is that along with the technology and the flexibility of the workday comes the expectation that employees are "open for business" during off hours. What employees thought was an option has now become the new norm. If you want to be a member of the team, you are expected to keep your smart phone in readiness and say goodbye to the good old nine to five workday. For those who live by the "To Do" list, your life itself may become one as well – an endless one that expands your working day and shrink your personal life. You must take action to prevent this from happening.

**Managing your email.**
Handling email is one activity that you must control if you are going to master technology. It seems to be increasing exponentially for everyone in my workshops. Most participants claim it consumes well over two hour a day. With the mobility of today's workforce and work itself being more a state of mind than a place that you go to, self-discipline and self-structure are more important than ever. The age of speed has people accepting as inevitable cell phones ring during lunch hours, text messages arriving at night and email popping up while watching your son's baseball game. We are allowing technology to control us, rather than the other way around.

Unfortunately to change this requires will power or self-discipline. I say unfortunately, because self-discipline is not something that comes naturally to most people. Most people don't accept responsibility for the impact speed is having on their lives. They blame it on the email, or cell phones that keep interrupting them. It's as though it's impossible to ignore email or turn off the cell phone or to schedule specific times to review messages. They think that life is something that happens to them rather than something that happens because of them. So the first step in controlling our time and our lives is to accept responsibility for what is happening to us – and to decide to change it. Self-discipline or self-control is simply the power to do something when it is easier not to do it. We all have the power but it's not exercised. The more you exercise it, the stronger it becomes. Self-discipline has a greater impact on how we manage our time than any other strategy. It is needed in order to form good habits, to defeat procrastination, stay organized, and to reap the benefits of delayed gratification. We must make small changes first. Don't make it difficult for yourself if you initially lack self-discipline. Build it gradually. For example, if you're checking email consistently throughout the day, decide to check it four or five times a day, at specific times. Say, first thing in the morning, mid-morning, noon, mid-afternoon and evening. Once you have a routine, cut out the early morning, evening and Sunday sessions – and so on – until you have complete control. You will tend to cheat a little at first, and backslide, and that's OK. You are building a habit, and if you persist, it will become easier to maintain self-discipline. Schedule specific times to review your email. Work on that one suggestion, and you will be strengthening your self-discipline at the same time. Schedule enough time to actually dispense with your email messages, not just quickly review them. Assume you check email ten times per day, spending ten minutes each time for a total of one hour, forty minutes. During this time let's say you can handle 50 emails – either replying, deleting, forwarding etc. Instead, if you check your email four times a day, and spend 20 minutes each time, for a total of 1 hour, 20 minutes, during this total time you would probably be able to handle the same 50 emails. But you have done it in 20 minutes less time. No matter how small the task, there is a setup time. You have a setup time for both the email (opening the program, clicking in the inbox etc.) and for resuming the task that you interrupted in order to check email. The fewer times you check email, the more time you save. An added benefit is that you won't be telling people by your actions that you respond instantly to every email you get. If you do, they will expect it. We train people how to treat us by our actions and habits. Control your email and you will go a long way to controlling your time. You will be eliminating a large source of stress and getting out of a reactive mode.

Timothy Ferriss in his book, *The 4-Hour Workweek* , claims he checks his email no more than once per week. He insists that any lost orders or other problems are overshadowed by his gain in efficiency. Personally, I wouldn't go to this extreme. But two or three times a day does not seem unreasonable. It's not generally a good idea to check email first thing in the morning. You could easily get distracted from your plan. Make sure you get your top priority done first. I recommend that you schedule one or more priority tasks each morning and not check your email until about 11:30. You could check it again about 3:30 in the afternoon. You might want to turn off the automatic send/receive option so that email doesn't pop up in your inbox the moment you sign on. Email programs seem to be designed to control *us* rather than the other way around. I encourage everyone to at least give it a try. Check your email twice per day for at least a couple of days and then assess the impact on your business. I'm sure most people have experienced a computer crash or an Internet access problem or a vacation when accessing email was impossible, and yet have survived the experience with no earth-shattering problems. When you *do* check your email, make sure that you have enough time to dispense with all the email messages in your inbox. You might want to allow a half hour for instance every time you check your email. Either delete it, forward it to someone else for reply, file it, answer it, move it to an action file or To Do list, or (if it warrants it) schedule time in your planner to take the necessary action before replying. It's a similar process you would use with paper. Handle it only once where possible and never leave it in the inbox.

**What is your Reactive Ratio?**

Do you respond to a lot more email messages than you originate? Are you deleting emails unanswered or unread? Are you spending so much time reacting to email that you don't have time for creativity, relaxation and renewal? If so, calculate your "Reactive Ratio." Count the total number of email messages you receive during a day. Include spam, egroup messages and newsletters whether you still read them or not. Divide the total number of incoming email messages by the number that you send during the day. The resulting ratio should be as low as possible.. You can easily calculate this ratio if you don't delete or move anything until the end of the day – even those that you have answered. The next morning, quickly count the total number of emails received the previous day as well as those sent the same day. If the ratio is high, take action by cancelling newsletters that you seldom read, get off egroups you don't participate in, place spam filters at higher levels, and get off mailing lists. Consider using a different email address for purchases to avoid spam. Watch your outgoing messages as well. Question whether all incoming messages require a reply. For instance, don't thank people for thanking you. Consider adding "No reply necessary" to many of your outgoing messages. And investigate apps such as unroll.me. The messages you originate also consume time and generate incoming messages. So question whether a quick phone call is better. Don't copy people unnecessarily. Even more important than your "Reactive Ratio" is the total time you spend on email each day. Keep messages brief. Use text replacement software for longer & repetitive replies such as instructions or directions. Allocate specific times to check and respond to email. This could be one hour late morning and one hour late afternoon. If you can get by with less time, so much the better. But don't fragment your day by checking email every few minutes or every hour.

**Write email messages with your purpose in mind.**

Many managers receive over 100 email messages per day, and spend only a second or two deciding whether to open them. Most such decisions are based on the subject line. Even when they open the message, they may only read a line or two before deleting it and going on to the next one. If you take the time to send an email message, take the time necessary to insure it fulfills its purpose. For instance, craft the subject line so it grabs their attention while telling them what the email message is about. Put the vital information in the first few lines and be clear and direct about what you want them to do after reading the message. Proof the message before sending it, correcting any typos and bad grammar, and tightening up the sentences. It may take longer to write shorter messages but they will get better results. Avoid attachments if possible. Instead, cut and paste the additional information at the end of the message. Make it is easy for the reader. Their time is just as valuable as your time, and you are the one who is initiating the interruption.

# KEEP YOUR LIFE IN BALANCE

Life balance is the process of working at all areas of your life: work, family, social, personal and spiritual so you can enjoy life and fulfill all your roles without experiencing undue stress. You can be a good parent, spouse, friend, and boss, with a healthy outlook, healthy body, and healthy mind. Life balance does not refer to a 9 to 5 workday where you spend 8 hours per day at work and no more. It simply means a *blend* of work and personal life that is satisfying to the individual and his or her family or significant others. Your personal life could be out of balance as well. You could be spending an inappropriate amount of time on a hobby, TV, surfing the Internet, golf or any number of activities. Balance has its rewards. It reduces stress and provides greater intrinsic rewards, such as a sense of satisfaction and peace of mind. Executives who give equal weight to work and personal life feel more successful at work, are less stressed, and have an easier time managing the demands of their work and personal lives.

**Signs your life is getting out of balance**

Lives usually get out of balance over a period of time, either through poor working habits, a reluctance to say no, a lack of planning, lack of goals or personal policies, or a failure to prioritize. Signs could include such things as a lack of sufficient sleep, uncompleted tasks, skipped lunches, rushing, stress, missed family activities, and so on. A common sign is when work starts infringing on other areas of your life, such as family, friends, and recreation. The most obvious sign that your life is out of balance is the amount of time spent on work-related activities. Working overtime on a regular basis is an indicator of imbalance. A Canadian Health report (From the book, *Sleep to be Sexy, Smart & Slim* by Ellen Michaud with

Julie Bain) claims that more than a half of all employees take work home, 69% check their email from home, 59% check voice mail after hours, 30% get work-related faxes, and 29% keep their cell phones on day and night. As a result, 46% feel that this work-related intrusion is a stressor and 44% report negative spillover onto their families. And the families are supposed to be the most effective buffer to workplace stress. Work is no longer a place, but a state of mind. And with BlackBerrys, cell phones and other PDAs, it's easier to be a workaholic these days. Eating on the run, taking your *BlackBerry* to the beach, being consistently late for personal and business events, not having enough time to exercise are all indicators of a lack of balance.

### Ways to maintain balance in your life

Maintaining balance involves gaining and maintaining control of your time and your life. This means that you should set goals in all the significant areas of life, simplify your life as much as feasible, schedule time for personal and family activities as well as those other areas of importance to you in addition to work-related activities. Life balance involves making wise choices. To balance your life you have to examine your personal values and what is really important in your life. Schedule time for the people, events and activities that are most important to you. You could keep track of your daily activities for a few weeks to find out how much time you are actually spending on the different activities. If one or more things consume a disproportionate amount of your time, then you can fix that by drawing up a personal time budget for yourself. Planning is important in order to avoid impulse spending of time. Plan what TV programs you will watch, the sporting events you will attend, the family outings and so on. Block off your vacations, evening classes, church activities, your child's baseball games, those scheduled dates with your spouse, those special events, that annual cruise or camping trip. Sometimes you may have to schedule personal activities during work time and work activities during personal time. Balance is a blend of work and personal life; there's no guarantee that one won't intrude on the other – but it usually balances out.

### Juggling a career, home and family

Some people are running a home-based business and have different challenges than those who commute to an office on a daily basis; but either way, you must adapt strategies that will keep your life in balance. These could involve delegating to family members, outsourcing some of the household tasks, enlisting the help of your spouse, streamlining procedures, eliminating unnecessary tasks, simplifying your life, organizing the home and office, being creative and taking shortcuts.

### Simplifying your life

The more stuff people own, the more time it demands. Many people could get rid of half their possessions and never miss them. They could also rid themselves of many of the activities in which they are involved and reduce the amount of time they spend on the remaining activities. Buy a bigger house and it may provide more space and comfort, but it also provides a larger mortgage, more taxes, a greater fear of robbery, more housework, and more expenses. It does not necessarily make one happier.

### Ways to simplify your life

- Realize you have the right to say no. Recognize that every time you say yes to somebody else, you are saying no to yourself and are depriving yourself of things that you want to accomplish.

- Stop doing non-priority tasks. Delegate them, outsource them, or eliminate them.

- Limit the number of friends you socialize with on a regular basis. Have more family get-togethers.

- Cancel your membership in associations that do little to further your career or personal development.

- Get rid of unnecessary credit cards; consolidate debt where practicable; and set up a schedule to reduce personal debt to zero.

- Build up reserves of space, time, and money so that you can base career decisions on your goals and beliefs instead of on immediate financial concerns.

- Intentionally spend your time, money, and energy on things that are important to you and not on every little thing that gets your attention.

- De-clutter your home and office. Get rid of everything you haven't worn, used, or referred to in more than a year.

- Introduce at least one timesaving strategy into your life each week, whether it be paying bills by automatic withdrawal, organizing the items in the medicine cabinet, or introducing technology to your workstation.

- Cancel subscriptions to magazines, journals, or newspapers that you seldom read.

- Cut in half the time you spend watching TV. Choose the programs you want to watch. Never sit in front of the TV with no objective in mind.

- Keep track of your spending habits for at least one month. Stop buying things you don't need. Draw up a personal budget and stick to it.

- Start scheduling personal activities into your planner, such as vacations, sporting events, recreational activities, physical fitness, and movie nights.

- Prioritize your *To Do* list, and delegate the bottom half.

- Don't save money if it means wasting time. Time is more valuable than money. Driving across town to get a bargain is no bargain. Similarly clipping coupons, washing your car, etc.

- Consume less. Repair items instead of buying new ones. Buy fewer upgrades.

- Do less entertaining. Take more walks, hikes, and time for yourself.

- Drive less. Locate closer to work if necessary.

- Cut your spending by at least 10%.

- Each week, ask yourself, "what can I do this week to simplify my life?"

**Don't put off living**

Most professionals working longer hours and investing more time in their careers. Work now and enjoy later seems to be the mantra of many of us. This simply doesn't work. Don't put off living or you will be too old too fully enjoy it. Work-life balance requires that we budget our time, not just our money. A deadline on our workday promotes efficiency. There is little relationship between time and efficiency. The more time you have to get your work done, the greater the tendency to waste it. If you get into the habit of working overtime, you are simply extending your current inefficiency to cover more hours of the day and intruding on personal and family time in the process. Instead, get organized, use technology, prioritize, schedule and practice sound time management principles during a pre-determined number of hours each day. Use the balance of the day for recreation, renewal and personal pursuits. Balance in itself will reduce stress, enhance creativity and improve efficiency during the "work" period of your day. The big payoff will be in the knowledge that you are not putting off until later, things that can be experienced and enjoyed in the present.

# PART 2: HOW TO ORGANIZE

# TIME MANAGEMENT & ORGANIZATION

Organizing is the act of rearranging *items* that are in a disorganized, cluttered state so that everything can be retrieved quickly with less effort, maximizing both their utility and visual appeal. Time management refers to increasing both the *efficiency and the effectiveness* of individuals and organizations through the organization of *tasks and events* by using tools such as planners and computers, and techniques and processes such as goal-setting, planning and scheduling. The two activities are interrelated since disorganization normally wastes time. The major difference between *organizing* and t *ime management* is that, in general, organizing deals with *things* and time management deals with *activities* that have a time dimension. Both are important. Time management in any environment, electronic or otherwise, involves working both efficiently and effectively. You are working efficiently when you complete tasks in the best possible way. You are working effectively when you concentrate your efforts on the best possible tasks. What you do is considered more important than how you do it. But when you get organized and work both efficiently and effectively, you are approaching excellence. Organization is our passport to productivity and time management is the vehicle that takes us there.

## THE VALUE OF TIME

The three major resources that are necessary in order to operate a successful business are time, money, and people. If you lose money, you can always earn or borrow more. If you lose people, you can re-hire. But if you lose time, you can never regain it – neither by working nor by borrowing. It is lost forever. And the sad part is, there is not an inexhaustible supply. You can dip into the time bank only so many times – then, once it's all gone, you're gone. It stands to reason that since time is in great demand and it is in such limited supply, that next to your health, it is your most valuable resource. Therefore, if you want to be successful in business and in life, you must learn to manage the time at your disposal. Unfortunately, some people can't even manage their money, let alone their time. And even those who *do* manage their money well do a relatively *poor* job of managing their time. The expression, "Look after the pennies and the dollars will look after themselves" is equally true for this precious commodity called time. We cannot afford to be spendthrifts when it comes to time. Spending time on impulse items such as dawdling over junk e-mail, thumbing through magazines, rearranging furniture and repositioning paintings when there are meaningful tasks to be performed is one way we can squander valuable minutes, which soon amount to hours. We also waste time by constantly shuffling papers, searching for misplaced items, interrupting ourselves and others needlessly, procrastinating on jobs that *must* be done eventually, worrying about things we can't control, and saying "yes" to time-consuming activities that do not relate to our goals. Add to this perfectionism, idle time, and a myriad of bad habits, and we have the potential to waste hours each day – hours that would be spent on profit-generating activities, family time, or self-renewal.

**GETTING ORGANIZED**

Usually the first step in gaining control of your time is to get organized. Organize your office, your files and your procedures to eliminate those wasted minutes searching for things, shuffling papers and interrupting others. Then look for shortcuts when performing those necessary but routine activities such as checking e-mail, chairing meetings, and fielding phone calls. The resulting time savings can then be invested in those profit-generating activities and personal priorities. Getting organized and time management are not one-time events. They are continuing processes of changing time wasting habits, streamlining the necessary activities, and focusing always on those key activities that generate the greatest return. Time management and organization can be viewed as common sense; but common sense not consistently practised. It may seem easy. But it isn't easy; because we are forced to change working habits that we have developed over the years. It takes motivation, determination, and perseverance. But the rewards, a more productive and satisfying life, are worth the effort.

**HOW DO WE BECOME SELF-MOTIVATED?**

Some people shrug off their disorganization by claiming they were born that way. Others claim they are so organized they were born on their due dates. But personal organization is not hereditary. You acquire your habits, good or bad, as you grow older. The more bad habits you have acquired, the more difficult it is to get organized; but it *can* be done. That's the good news. The bad news is it takes effort. Nothing worthwhile comes easily. Anyone can resolve to get up a half hour earlier, for example; but actually getting up requires effort. It takes varying degrees of effort to put things back after using them, purge files, develop the "do it now" habit, and tear yourself away from pleasant but non-productive tasks. So you must want to get organized badly enough to endure some temporary awkwardness. You must be self-motivated. No seminar, book, or DVD is ever going to give you the incentive to persist in your efforts to get organized. That's a fact that you must accept. So where does the motivation come from? Motivation is a product of the amount of desire to get organized multiplied by the expectancy that you will succeed. So if you are experiencing few problems the way you are, and are happy with the results you are achieving, you will have a low desire to change. But if you are convinced that you can get more accomplished and lead a better life if you were more organized and time-effective, your desire will be high. It only remains that you are convinced that certain changes *will* lead to personal organization. And confirmation of that is available from individuals who have succeeded in changing habits and increasing their effectiveness.

**MAKE CHANGES GRADUALLY**

A word of caution: don't try to change too many things at once. Remember that getting organized, like time management, is a life-long process. Make changes gradually. Become comfortable with using a telephone log or follow-up file for example, before revamping the way you conduct yourself in other areas. Where do you get your ideas? There are hundreds of books on the topic of organization. Articles appear almost every month in one of the thousands of magazines and blogs being posted. There is no shortage of ideas on organizing and saving time. But what you must do is select those ideas you feel will work for you. Adapt them, if necessary, to suit your particular job or situation, then put them into practice.

**CONTROL THE THINGS YOU CAN CONTROL**

Time does not pass. We do. Don't try to control time or you will simply become frustrated. Time cannot be saved, stored, stopped, or stretched. So stop concentrating on *time* and focus your attention on something you *can* influence – *yourself.* Use time only as a measuring stick to determine how effective you can become. Can you increase the number of significant accomplishments within the same time frame? Or can you achieve what you are now achieving in a shorter period of time? Once you start concentrating on something you *can* control – *yourself* – your work *methods, tools a* nd work *environment,* you eliminate many of the frustrations experienced when you try to control others, or time itself over which you have little or no control. Many of the problems you were blaming on the clock – or others – disappear.

Ask yourself some basic questions:

*Do I have a clear set of personal goals* in *writing?*

Saving time is to no avail if you have nothing meaningful to spend it on. Examine yourself and your values. Determine what is important to you and what you would like to accomplish in your lifetime. Then, put these aspirations into the form of specific objectives that you can work towards.

*Do I use my planner properly?*

Use it to record more than people appointments and meetings; use it to plan your week in advance. Jot down specific days and times when you plan to work on that project, report, article, sales call or counseling session. Fill your planner with priorities that relate to your goals so there's no room for the trivia.

*Am I writing things down instead of relying on my memory?*

Many ideas and opportunities are lost, mistakes made, and communications stifled simply because we relied on our memories. Always carry a notepad or PDA with recording capability with you. Take notes on telephone calls, actions resulting from meetings, ideas that pop into your head, assignments given and received, deadline dates and dates of events such as birthdays, conferences, and reviews.

*Am I procrastinating?*

Many people have goals that are really only intentions. Because they never get around to working on them. They are sidetracked by those urgent but unimportant activities that seemingly must be done. Or they gravitate towards those pleasant or easy tasks that consume their time. Reducing procrastination is essential if you are to lead a fruitful life and achieve a sense of accomplishment.

*Am I a packrat?*

Are you among the many people in this country who are drowning in their possessions? Do you have drawers, files, and cabinets filled with things you never use? Paperwork alone is still a real problem for many people. It is difficult to be organized when there is simply too much to organize. ( *Organize your work, home & life*)

*Do I work in a disorganized environment?*

People waste valuable time searching for things, shuffling papers, interrupting themselves, and jumping from one job to another simply because their work area is disorganized. Spend a day – or evening – cleaning out your desk drawers, eliminating unnecessary paperwork, developing a simple file system, follow-up file and project files. Decide where you will store each item and stick to it. Stop using the desk top as a storage area, clear out your in-basket daily, and take the few seconds necessary to put away a project once you have finished working on it for the time being. You will work better if you are organized. ( *Organize your work, home & life*)

*Am I creating a work environment that maximizes my energy, productivity and creativity?*

Until recently, most people have ignored such things as natural lighting, greenery, colors, music and other factors (besides the physical layout and organization) that have an impact on personal productivity, health and well-being. Take advantage of the facts revealed by research that will positively impact your success by keeping up to date on these areas and making changes where applicable.

*Am I working smarter rather than harder?*

Are you using up valuable time on jobs that can be delegated, assigned, or contracted out to others? You have a limited amount of time; it never varies. So make sure you fill it with those priority activities that only you can perform. For example, don't spend three hours of your life washing your car when you can have it done for you for sixty Rands. (Unless, of course, your time is not worth twenty Rands per hour, or there's nothing else you'd rather do than wash cars.) Always search out better ways of doing things.

*Am I caught up in the tyranny of the urgent?*

If you keep yourself busy enough you won't notice that you're not accomplishing anything. Are you constantly under time pressures, fighting to keep your head above water? You must divorce yourself from the rat race, modify your sense of time urgency, and concentrate on the 20% of the activities that produce 80% of the results.

# GET ORGANIZED

Organization aids peace of mind, creativity, and attention as well as time effectiveness. Disorganization, on the other hand, causes stress, fractured thinking and wasted time. It could even contribute to obesity. For example, a *Psychology Today* article posted on May 17, 2017 mentioned a study showing that people will eat more cookies and snacks if working in a messy and disorganized kitchen. A special edition of *Mindfulness* , April, 2017, reported that according to the recent study published in *Environment and Behavior* , we are likely to overeat up to 34% more when our kitchens are in a mess – such as old newspapers, unopened mail on the counter and so on. Mehmet Oz and Mike Roizen, authors of *YOU: On a Diet* , claim that visual clutter slows down the brain. They say that's why clusters of road signs double the chances of missing the one you're looking for. It also explains why website designers aim for simplicity. So clearing clutter from your desk, office and home and leaving more wide open spaces also helps to clear your mind so it will be more productive. As we read more about the workings of our brain, we learn even more about the importance of getting organized. According to neuroscientist Torkel Klingberg, author of *The overflowing brain* , mental clutter is a suspect in the cause of age-related memory losses. Clearing clutter from your desk, office and home and leaving more wide open spaces also helps to clear your mind so it will be more productive. To stay organized you must develop systems unique to your situation, whether it is handling paperwork, managing email, conducting meetings, using a follow-up file or scheduling in a planner. D eciding in advance when you will do something increases your commitment to do it. That's one of the reasons I suggest to people that they block off times in their planner to actually do the priority tasks. This could include blocks of time to organize specific areas of your home and office.

### *Re-purpose storage space*

When you sort through your belongings and donate or scrap the sweaters, blouses, scarves and other clothing items you never use, re-purpose the drawer for those non-clothing items that are causing your closets and other storage areas to overflow. You are re-purposing when you remove bottom shelves of linen closets to store your golf clubs or use a kitchen drawer to house your toolkit. Don't feel that you have to use all storage areas for the purpose they were originally intended. I use a spare bedroom as an office, and the closet organizers such as hanging compartments designed for shoes and larger ones for sweaters now house my various office supplies.

### *Not so junky junk drawer*

I maintain that everyone needs a junk drawer for miscellaneous one-of-a-kind items. The secret is not to let it expand into two or more junk drawers. When items that you just can't part with become too plentiful to find quickly, add dividers to the drawer to separate items that have some common association – such as those used in the same room (kitchen, garden, etc.), or for common use (cooking, repairing, washing, etc.).

### *Act at the time of recall*

When you recall that you need to mail letters in the morning or deposit clothes for dry cleaning or return a book to a friend, act now, not in the morning. Place those items near the front door or on the front car seat – where they won't be missed. Marking them on a "To Do" list might not allow enough time if you're rushing in the morning. And you could even misplace or forget to look at your "To Do" list.

*Organizing tip for procrastinators*

Not ready to part with some of the items cluttering up your home or office? In addition to your "Toss", "Keep", and "Donate" boxes, have a fourth one labelled "In limbo" for those items that you can't decide whether to toss, donate or keep. Six months or a year later, tackle this box as well. If you haven't needed, looked for, missed or even thought about any of the items in the meantime, it will be a lot easier to part with them.

*Brighten up those storage areas*

Rather than storing those extra paintings and framed photographs that usually get shoved under the bed, and that artificial plant that you received from Aunt Sally, use them to embellish closets, the laundry room and other out-of-sight areas that tend to attract unused stuff. You might hesitate before blocking wall-hangings and other decorative pieces. It also gives you the added advantage of brightening up those otherwise cluttered hideaway places that you have to visit frequently. It might even give your mood a boost. If you need a further reason to invest a little time in getting organized, how about this statistic published in the April 6, 2013 issue of *The Globe & Mail* in an article by Leah Etchler? A U.S Study found that employees lose 76 hours per year as a result of disorganization. That's time that could be put to use – either in your business or your personal life.

## DISORGANIZED? DON'T BLAME IT ON YOUR BRAIN

You were going to clean out that cupboard today, but a TV program came on that you didn't want to miss. And after all, if you miss this program it may never air again – and you can always clean the cupboard tomorrow. In the old days we used to call this procrastination – doing what you would rather do now and putting off the more important things until later.

But with all of the brain research going on today, it's now suggested that it's your brain that's at fault. The brain's default setting is "to tap the least tiring cognitive process," according to an article in the December, 2015 issue of *Scientific American Mind*. In other words, it takes the path of least resistance – the easiest and least energy-consuming route. It's certainly easier to leave something out than put it away or to do something later rather than now – including your intention to organize your home and office. We now have legitimate reasons for shirking our responsibilities, rationalizing our errors, and making snap decisions without examining the facts. With the advent of functional MRIs, and locating the regions of the brain responsible for everything from lack of willpower to angry outbursts, we can pinpoint the blame even further. "It's the insula or the dorsolateral prefrontal cortex," we might claim. We even have attorneys arguing in court rooms that their clients were not responsible for their crimes since it was some malfunction of a certain region of their brain. What I have concluded personally is that the mind is separate from the brain. You are not your brain; you are your mind. Your brain is simply part of the body – your personal computer, which does your bidding. You can control your brain – unless this most complicated computer in the universe actually breaks down – so get ready to accept responsibility for at least most of your behaviours. Most of the brain books will confirm the neuroplasticity of the brain, and that you are able to reprogram it to develop willpower, resist impulses, overcome procrastination, and strengthen your planning and organizing skills, and so on. . You may not be your brain; but you are able to control it. As the title of one of those brain books urges, *change your brain; change your life*. As an example, there are many ways you can strengthen your executive skills – those brain-based skills that allow you to manage time, focus, persist, plan, resist impulses and maintain self-control, among other behaviors.

## ARE YOU DISORGANIZED?

You might consider your state of organization – or disorganization in your office or home, and take steps to improve it. Below is a brief quiz with 15 statements. Check off those statements that are true in your case. Then add up the number of checkmarks.

- I spend more than fifteen minutes each day searching for things.

- If all the paperwork on my desk were put into one pile it would be over two inches thick.

- I frequently misplace such things as car keys, eyeglasses, or other personal effects.

- When searching for something in a drawer, the drawer always looks messier when I'm finished.

- It's impossible for me to keep flat surfaces free from clutter. I collect things on top of spare desks, credenzas, filing cabinets, tables.

- We share such things as 3-hole punches and staplers at the office.

- Most common things, such as printer paper, stationery, and other office supplies are centrally located.

- It is sometimes difficult to locate things in the filing cabinets.

- I frequently spend five minutes or more searching for

files on my computer.

- I frequently store things without listing the items in each carton (or without keeping index cards of the contents).

- I don't keep a follow-up file for storing work in process.

- My in-basket is on my desk.

- At home or at work we store things in spots that we have not designated for them. Example, vacuum cleaner or golf clubs in hall closet, cartons of envelopes in coat closet, etc.

- I have more than one junk drawer in my desk/dresser/kitchen.

- In closets, stairwells, storage rooms, etc., we use floor space as much as we use racks, shelves and hangers.

If you checked off more than 5 statements as being true, you are disorganized to at last some extent and I recommend that you immediately block off some time in your planning calendar this week to get organized. As little as one hour each week will start paying dividends within a few weeks, and you will gain much more time than you invest. It's also important to have an organized office to minimize distractions, boost efficiency, lower stress, conserve energy and increase personal comfort while working on your priority tasks.

# HOW ORGANIZED IS YOUR OFFICE?

A survey conducted by Steelcase Canada quite some time ago revealed that 74 percent of office workers feel they could do more work in the same amount of time if office conditions were changed. The three factors office workers said could help them increase their productivity are improved work flow between people and departments, reduction of noise and distraction in the office, and access to proper job equipment. Choose a comfortable, sturdy adjustable chair that allows you to rest your feet on the floor while maintaining your eyes at about 30 inches from the computer screen with the top part of the monitor slightly below eye level. If you need a cushion to support your lower back, get one. Hopefully you will spend as much time on your feet or pacing around the office while you work since it is both healthier, and in many cases, more productive. Discourage interruptions by avoiding eye contact with passersby. Don't position your desk so you are facing an open doorway. You might place your desk to one side, so people will have to go out of their way to see you. If they are able to catch your eye from outside the office they will be tempted to walk inside and strike up a conversation. For the same reason, avoid having gathering spots outside your office such as a coffee area, water cooler or copying station. A coffee maker, for example, seems to put people in a socializing mood. That's okay if everyone takes their break at the same time, but this seldom happens. Although the absence of chairs would make unscheduled visitations brief, it could also make scheduled meetings more inconvenient. But don't have chairs close to your desk or facing you. They're an open invitation for people to slip into them. Instead, place them about ten feet or more from the desk or against a wall on either side of the room. When the drop-in approaches your desk, you can stand and remain standing until the brief conversation is over. If you want to carry on a lengthy conversation, simply move from your desk to the chairs and carry on the conversation in the open, facing each other, without the barrier of a desk between you. Have your office decorated tastefully, but simply. A lot of photos, trophies, certificates and citations will encourage chit chat. Don't have family photos or memorabilia in your line of sight. These could initiate the brain's impromptu trip down memory lane. A window view is okay as long as it's a view of nature and not a brick wall or a busy carnival. Don't have sofas if you don't sleep in your office. But plants are great, even if you don't garden. And a clock is a great reminder of the speed at which time passes; place it where your visitor can see it. Arrange your working tools and furniture closely around the desk area. Don't place frequently-used filing cabinets or bookcases on the other side of the room. You should have everything that you frequently use each day within reach. Have an adequate inventory of felt pens, paperclips, staples, highlighter markers, etc. in one of your desk drawers. Don't skimp on office supplies; have your own stapler, 3-hole punch, and whatever else you use frequently. Sharing with other people is not economical when you take lost time into consideration. Your desk does not have to be large, but you must have sufficient working area. The desk is not meant for storage, so keep it clear of paperwork except for projects you are working on. Other projects should be retained in a follow-up file; the bulkier ones can be kept in colored manila folders, clearly identified. These should be kept in hanging files in your desk drawer. If your desk doesn't have a drawer large enough to hold files, I recommend you get one that does. If this is impossible, keep the follow-up file system and project files in a vertical file holder on top of your desk or in a filing cabinet at the side of your desk. The follow-up file will be discussed later. Keep articles, procedures, job descriptions, policies, product bulletins and anything else that you refer to frequently in 3-ring binders. Label them clearly for easy identification; buy some self-adhesive insert holders for the spines of these binders. The bookcase should be within reach. Surround yourself on three sides with your working materials. Your office should be arranged so that everything is readily accessible. Every time you have to walk to another area for supplies, you risk an extended interruption. So anticipate the envelopes, letterhead, computer paper, etc., that you will need, and include them in your inventory. If you need an extra cabinet or shelf on the wall near your desk, get one. Have a set of stacking trays on your desk or credenza bearing the names of people who report to you, or who you communicate with on a regular basis. This could include your boss. Whenever there is something requiring their attention, jot notes on it and toss it in one of those trays. Invariably they will interrupt you at least once every day and they can empty their tray when they do. Don't deliver paperwork to anyone who will be dropping in. Save yourself some trips. Don't let your office environment control you. You spend too many hours there to suffer unnecessary inconveniences. If a floor receptacle prevents you from placing your desk where you want it, have the outlet moved. If the door opens the wrong way, have it changed. If the lighting is poor, add more lights. If the rollers on your chair are worn, replace them. Any costs incurred are one-time costs; the time savings are forever.

**GETTING RID OF THE BACKLOG**

In an office environment, people can become so overwhelmed with paperwork and so pressured by time constraints, that they feel it's impossible to keep on top of it all. They become packrats by default. If you find yourself buried in paperwork, have an overflowing in basket, a desk drawer crammed with files, reports and trivia and stacks of material on your credenza, window ledges and filing cabinets, you will have difficulty coping with current material. You must first get rid of the backlog, and organize yourself so the paperwork will never get ahead of you again. First you must clean up your desk, office, and files. Here is a ten-point system for getting rid of your backlog:

1. Block off a three-hour period in your planning calendar. If it's impossible during working hours, schedule it at night or on a weekend.

2. Empty all the desk drawers, ledges, etc., of paperwork. Don't tackle filing cabinets at this stage – only your desk, credenza, and any visible piles of paperwork.

3. Toss all paperwork into three envelope boxes marked "Priority", "Routine", and "Unimportant". Stack any magazines separately.

4. As you carry out Step 3, quickly scan the material and recycle anything that can be discarded.

5. One of the desk drawers should be a file drawer. If not, use a file cabinet drawer that is within reach of your desk. Install hanging folders.

6. Use 13 of the hanging folders, along with 31 manila folders, for a follow-up file. An example is described later. Label the other folders with titles of your major on-going projects. Every hanging file should contain a similarly labeled manila file folder.

7. One or more of your desk drawers will contain "non-paperwork" – miscellaneous paraphernalia and office supplies. Separate those items you actually *use* on a regular basis, and

organize them in an organizer tray. Retain in a shallow drawer.

8. Throw out whatever items your willpower will allow. Place the other items in a shoebox; label "Junk Drawer", followed by the date, and stash them away in some dark closet. Chances are you'll never need them again. Out of sight, out of mind, and eventually, out of the building.

9. Go through those envelope boxes, starting with the one labeled "Priority", dealing with each piece of paper as you pick it up. Scrap it, delegate it, do it, or schedule a time to do it later. In the latter case, block off time to do it in your planner, and put the paperwork in the follow-up file.

10. It is unlikely you will be able to dispense with all the paperwork in 3 hours. Set the boxes aside and dedicate at least a half-hour every morning to systematically go through this paperwork until it is all scrapped, done, delegated, or scheduled for a later time. This is in addition to the time you already spend on your incoming e-mail and other material. You need to keep on top of your incoming material so another backlog does not accumulate. Once the backlog has disappeared, you have that half-our back.

## ORGANIZE YOUR OFFICE FOR MAXIMUM PRODUCTIVITY

As mentioned, organize your desk and surrounding area so that frequently used materials and supplies and equipment are within reach. The less frequently you use materials, the farther away they should be stored. For example, writing materials might be on your desk with your computer, working files in your left hand desk drawer and archived files in another room entirely.

Here are a few additional tips for keeping your office and desk area organized:

- Use organizer trays in your most accessible desk drawers to house such items as elastic bands, sticky notes, scissors, tape, batteries, staples, thumb drives, monitor cleaner, postage stamps, scratch pads, labels, labels, forms, and so on. Keep like things close together but rarely in the same compartment of the organizer tray.

- Keep frequently-used hardcopy files in hanging folders in your desk's filing drawer or in a freestanding filing cabinet within reach. Action files such as this week's meeting material, invoices to be paid, information for an article being written or items to be reviewed can be held in a vertical step file device on your desk. But otherwise keep your desk as clear as possible to accommodate your current project and computer or laptop.

- Since people recognize color faster than they can decipher text, for your action folders it is usually a good idea to color code the various categories. Use different colored manila file folders and hanging folders to house the paperwork for different projects and categories. You might have red for action items, blue for payables, yellow for follow-ups, and so on. Of course the tabs should be clearly labelled as well; but eventually you won't even have to refer to the tab to identify the folder.

- To store inventory and supplies you could paint shelves different colors so you would know that electronic items, electrical cords etc. are on the white shelf, packaging materials on the green shelf, paper products on the yellow shelf, safety and first aid supplies on the red shelf, and so on. Color provides instant identification among similar items, and if you file by color, anything filed in the wrong place can be quickly spotted. I particularly like the idea of color-coding books according to topic so it is easy to file and retrieve by topic. This is explained later in this chapter.

- Whenever possible, store your supplies where they are used – printer paper, ink cartridges etc. near the printer, copier supplies near the copier and so on. These organizing principles apply to your digital files and forms as well. Have frequently used documents such as your weekly blog articles, tweets, monthly reports etc. in a folder on your computer desktop. Avoid having to click through five or six levels of document folders every day or week to reach the electronic files that you use every day.

- Less frequently used files can be several levels down in your main "Documents" folder. For instance, you might have to click through Documents, Associations, NAPO, Conferences, and Exhibits each year to reach the display information document.

- Don't allow your computer desktop to be cluttered with folders and individual documents. File newly created documents in the proper folder as you create them. Temporary storage easily becomes more permanent and slows the retrieval process.

- Have a bookcase within reach for more current books that you refer to frequently for research while writing articles, writing proposals for clients or developing training programs. Once they are referred to less frequently and replaced by more current books, move them to your larger bookcases farther from your immediate working area.

- Remove all clutter and other potential distractions from your immediate work area – including the in-basket on your desk if your office is in a company. Hopefully you have already decided what you will be working on each day and don't need additional distractions. Any in-basket should be outside your office or at least as close as possible to the doorway. If it's a crisis, people won't use your in-basket anyway.

- Don't run out of supplies or stationery. Organize the storage so there's a place for everything. Insist on everything being kept that way. For forms, letterhead, envelopes, promotion material, tape a copy to the outside of the box for easy identification. Number the cartons: 1, 2, 3, etc., when they come in. Stack them in reverse order and when you get down to 2 or 1, re-order.

- Have written procedures for all tasks. Have the staff members who are responsible for the tasks make up the procedures. Review them. Refine them. Simplify them if possible. And make everyone in the office aware of them.

- Get a large wall calendar. Record all meetings, conferences, workshops, vacations, important deadlines, so everyone can see them.

**THE FOLLOW-UP FILE**

A clear desk does not guarantee that you'll be organized. But it helps. If you have a handful of material relating to a project and nowhere to put it, don't leave it on your desk or toss it back into the in-basket. Either place it in the appropriate Action File or into a follow-up file, which schedules it on a particular date. When you put something in your follow-up file for a particular date, be sure to block off enough time in your planner to actually work on it – unless it simply requires a quick phone call or something requiring a few minutes only. The follow-up file is exclusive of your assistant's follow-up file (if you have an administrative assistant). If your staff member keeps a follow-up file and uses it to jog your memory on reports due, or items for approval, that's great. But this is *your* personal follow-up file, which contains the back-up material you will need for those tasks that you have scheduled in your time planner to do personally. Place paperwork into this follow-up file when a time to complete it has been blocked off in your planning calendar. The follow-up file system consists of thirteen hanging files marked January, February, etc., and the last one marked "Next year". One set of manila folders marked from 1 to 31, corresponding to the days of the month is placed in the current month's hanging folder. There is only one set of manila folders for the current month only. At the first of the month when you have emptied the day's project papers, you then move that manila folder to the next month's hanging folder and it becomes the first of the next month. All 31 folders keep rotating through the monthly hanging folders. I have a portable file system that can travel with me if I have to work elsewhere, and the files can quickly be transferred to a desktop file holder if it is more convenient to do so. It is pictured below. This follow-up file system is simply an adjunct to your time planner. Your planner contains your work plan. When you arrive in the morning, flip open your time planner and if you see a report scheduled for 9:00 a.m., you know exactly where to look for the back-up papers needed – in that day's follow-up file. hanging folders for easy retrieval. Even though they are labelled, you will soon get to know that the red folder is "A" project, the green folder the "B" project, and so on.

## ORGANIZING YOUR BOOKS

Use a system that feels comfortable and lends itself to the way you work. I prefer my books organized by topic rather than by author or title. Perhaps this is due to the fact that I spend a large portion of my time writing. I rarely search for a specific book because I am more interested in a specific topic. It's more important for me to be able to quickly locate all the books on one topic. So for my thousand or more books I keep the topics together and use a color coding method to quickly spot the different topics. I apply small self-adhesive labels to the bottom of the spines, a different color for each topic. For example, orange for those dealing with the brain, dark green for business, red for technology, blue for meetings, and so on. When the book covers more than one topic in depth, I would add a label for the other major topics as well, always keeping the predominant topic label at the bottom. It would be filed in that section. Since I am interested in the predominant topic rather than the book title, I don't apply a label until I have at least skimmed through the book. If you have a lot of topics you could easily run out of colors. But you can always vary the size, shape or shade of the label so they are easily distinguishable. For example I use dark green for business and light green for self-development. I also use larger white square labels for time management, my main topic of interest. The colored label will allow you to quickly return the book to its assigned location on the shelf and to spot any that have been misfiled. See the photo below. Have a bookcase within reach for more current books that you refer to frequently for research or guidance. As you refer to them less frequently you can always move them to your larger bookcases farther from your immediate working area, and replace them with your newer purchases. It is a real time saver when you don't have to get up every few minutes to fetch a book from some far-away bookcase. So I have a rotating bookcase within reach for the most frequently used books – in addition to the reachable ones on the wall to my right and the others that are located some distance away. Since I generally write in 90-minute increments of time. I want to maximize my use of this limited segment of time. A plastic floor plate and chair on rollers allows me to access materials quickly while still in my chair. When removing a book from your library shelves, you might consider pulling the next one a few out a few inches so it protrudes from the rest. Then you can then quickly return it to its exact location – although I don't find this saves much time unless you are frequently accessing the same book. Paperback books waste a lot of space on the standard 12-inch deep bookshelf. Double up and conserve precious space by storing the books two layers deep. In order to see the back row of books, put two 2 × 4's, one on top of the other, on the back of the shelf to function like a stair step. This will raise the back row four inches and enable you to see and choose the book you need. I work in a home office. One of the bedrooms is repurposed as an office with a clothes closet repurposed as a storage room and clothes and shoe organizers, a bookcase and hangers within the closet repurposed as supply holders and shelving. I mentioned organizer trays in this chapter. Below are a couple of photos showing two of my desk drawers. You can get trays in many sizes and various numbers, sizes and shapes of compartments. Did I organize them for these photos? Absolutely. Only slightly. But I didn't photograph my junk drawer, which I feel everyone needs. It is the junk drawer that allows me keep the other drawers organized. It is cleaned out only a few times a year. Don't spend so much time organizing that you neglect the important things in business and in life. But it's worthwhile investing a day or so to completely organize your home and office. Then it requires very little time on a daily basis to keep it that way. Don't be discouraged if you slip once in awhile. It gets easier as you continue to work at it. And organization is not the goal. Efficiency and effectiveness is the goal.

## ORGANIZE YOUR ELECTRONIC FILES

Just as a messy desk wastes time, so does a messy desktop computer. Although a cluttered screen may not look as physically cluttered as a messy closet, basement or garage, it can be just as great a time waster. With the proliferation of emails, downloads, documents, articles and e-books, time is easily wasted accessing the various items on file – especially if you have filed them in haste or left them on your desktop. By now, you should have a better idea of the major categories (folders) and topics (sub-folders) that you will need, and you're in a better position to give them more descriptive titles. So drag all the existing files into a folder labeled "OLD FILES," and start a new filing system. When you do have to search through these old files for something, transfer it into your new organized filing system once you find it. Probably 90% of your old files will remain untouched. From now on take the time to file your documents at the time that you create, receive or download them. Don't file on the desktop, even temporarily. The "do it now" habit works for filing as well as for tasks. If you have to take action on something before filing or deleting it, save it temporarily in an "ACTION" folder. This becomes your electronic "To Do" folder. When placing anything in this action folder, it should be listed on the "To Do" section in your planner as well so you will be reminded to take action at the right time. If necessary, rename any documents that you receive so they will be properly identified and able to be found quickly. This especially applies to email since many people fail to identify the topic with an adequately descriptive header – if they use a header at all. Also, when you receive the revised copies or final versions of anything, be sure to delete the ones they are replacing. Keep your desktop free of icons and shortcuts for programs you rarely use. Drag them into a "Programs" folder and leave visible only those that you use on a recurring basis. While you're at it, uninstall completely any programs you never use. You might also have a Friday afternoon or Monday morning "cleanup" session where you pick a folder and delete any files that you haven't referred to in a few years and are unlikely to do so.

# MERGING TIME & ORGANIZATION

Don't plan your office as though you were going to be sitting all day. It's unhealthy, non-productive and downright dangerous.

An article aptly titled *Killer chairs*, which appeared in the November, 2014 issue of Scientific American, the book, *Eat Move Sleep*, by Tom Rath, and various independent studies provide statistics that should convince everyone that any office should be conducive to physical movement, whether it involves a stand-up desk or freedom to move about the office while working. For example,

- Those sitting for over four hours a day watching TV had a 46% increase in deaths from any cause than those spending less than two hours a day.

- Sitting for more than half the day doubles the risk of diabetes and cardiovascular problems.

- Obese people sat 2.25 hours longer than their lean counterparts every day, and expended 350 fewer calories.

- Research at the *University of California* long ago showed that people digest complex facts better and make quicker decisions when standing. Some actually absorbed information 40% faster.

- Studies reported in the August 27, 2016 issue of *Toronto Star* show that giving kids standing desks in school helps them burn more calories and improves behavioural classroom engagement.

- One 2013 Australian survey of 63,048 middle-aged

men found that those who sat for more than four hours a day were more likely to have a chronic disease like high blood pressure and heart disease, diabetes, and cancer.

- Sitting at a desk five days a week could compress your spine, degenerate your muscles, and according to at least a few reports, even cause depression or cancer.

Your office should allow you to walk around while you talk on the phone, work at a stand-up desk, have stand-up meetings, take the stairs instead of the elevator, and periodically go for a brief walk – anything that will get you out of your chair during the day.

You might consider alternating between a stationary desk and a standing desk. Experiment to see what type of work is best done sitting, standing or while walking around the office. And don't forget the advantage of spending time in another location altogether, such as at a picnic bench or in a coffee shop.

**PRODUCTIVITY REVISITED**

Ever since I broadened my field of interest to include holistic time management, I have been amazed at how many factors influence our productivity besides the usual efficiency – organizing – planning triad of strategies. I have written about them in previous books – everything from music to physical movement, from office greenery to window scenery and from colors to coffee shops. In the process of doing all this, I've been forced to modify my narrow definition of personal productivity. In the past I have defined personal productivity solely in business terms, such as output per unit of input, whether that is the number of invoices processed per hour or the number of customers served in a day or the number of tasks completed during the week. Other business writers all seem to do the same thing – define personal productivity in terms of the volume of work-related output, which presumably will assist corporate productivity as long as the individual is productive in a direction that aligns with corporate goals.

The problem with this approach is that it does not allow for a truly "personal" output, which may or may not have anything to do with corporate efficiency or productivity. For example, it has been shown that nature walks, friendships, and volunteering can all help, either directly or indirectly, to increase work-related productivity. But they can also have other beneficial outputs such as happiness, hope and well-being, which may or may not influence work-related productivity one iota. And yet who can deny the possible personal benefits of such things, including mental health, mindfulness, and empathy and so on.

**CORPORATE PRODUCTIVITY VS. PERSONAL PRODUCTIVITY**

What I choose to do, therefore, is have two distinct definitions; one for personal productivity and another for corporate or work-related productivity. Corporate productivity is a term I will use for the volume of output per unit of input, such as the number of widgets for hour. It is solely a measure of the efficiency of production, whether by an individual or team. Corporate productivity can be increased by increasing the output without increasing the input or increasing output drastically with only a slight increase in input. This might be accomplished through the use of technology or by workers simply working smarter and more efficiently.

Personal productivity can then be defined as the value of your personal life in terms of quality, quantity and contribution. Personal productivity might be increased through varying inputs, such as social relationships, an active lifestyle, love, forgiveness, and a continuing relationship with nature. The personal productivity of an individual in most cases will have a positive influence on corporate productivity if the person is involved in a business or career; but that is not necessarily the case. The challenge is to balance the two. The tendency in the workplace is to increase input rather than change input. For example, the impulse is to work harder, even though it has been shown that the top performers tend to work no more than 4.5 hours a day. And how many people would actually think to get more sleep in order to get more done? But with an equal focus on personal productivity, which relies heavily on health and lifestyle issues, it's easier to buffer the traditional methods of increasing corporate productivity, which are driven solely by efficiency and achievement. This will insure that not only the company will gain in terms of increased productivity, but the individual will gain as well in terms of personal growth, fulfillment, and physical, mental and spiritual well-being.

### ADVANTAGES OF A WRITTEN "TO DO" LIST

A digital list of "things to do" on your computer or laptop can becomes long and unmanageable, with a mixture of priority and less important and trivial items, some of which must be done immediately and others later on – or even months into the future. This tends to increase your anxiety level, serves as a distraction, and wastes time as you constantly scan the items to decide which ones to work on that day. These decisions consume energy that otherwise could be spent on priority tasks. You can manage your "to do" list more effectively by separating it from your computer workstation as a handwritten list. Then you can choose a few of the most important items (depending on the time they will take) and record them in your daily planner or Daily Priority Pad, crossing them off your master list as you do so. It's important that you don't choose too many items each day. Always allow up to 50% more time than you think the task will take – or plan for only four or five hours of real work each day. The balance of the work day will be filled by unplanned tasks and activities that inevitably occur. One advantage of the planning calendar over the priority pad is that you can actually schedule a block of time for each task and have a visual view of the times that are still available for other work. But be careful not to over schedule your day. Writing down your "to do" list frees up working memory, imprints the items in your mind, allows time to evaluate their importance, and provides a motivational sense of accomplishment as you cross off each item. Mikael Cho, cofounder of Crew, claimed that "the separation from the digital space (where I do most of my work) to the physical, helped me feel less overwhelmed." Physically writing things down also increases your focus on what you are doing at the time, avoids mental multitasking, and helps you to make a better decisions when selecting the priorities for each day. I personally use the To Do sections (referred to as "Weekly action items") in my *Taylor Planner* since this allows me to assign items to specific weeks. The Daily Priority Pad (for those who don't necessarily use a paper planner) allows you to assign them to specific days. I recommend you use whatever system works best for you. This includes a smartphone since everything mentioned here can be done electronically – although there are advantages to maintaining good old-fashioned cursive handwriting for some activities.

### ARE PAPER PLANNERS MAKING A COMEBACK?

Don't toss out your paper planner just yet. It appears that using both a smartphone and a paper planner is gaining in popularity.

Michael Grothhaus, a novelist, freelance journalist, wrote an article for the April 4, 2017 issue of *Fast Company* titled, "*What happened when I ditched my smartphone for a paper planner.*" Of course he didn't really ditch his smartphone, but he used a paper planner for writing down his tasks and mapping out his intentions and reminders. He discovered that a trend was beginning to develop (among younger people no less) to revert to paper planners – probably reinforced by research that backs up what we paper planner advocates experienced over the years – that writing things down improves memory and recall of the items. It also creates order in your mind and you can recall the sequence of things you must do, and the relative importance and urgency of the items. Flipping back and forth through the pages keeps you on track and the cursive note-taking is tonic for the brain. The writer of the above article quotes Anjali Khosla, editor of *Fast Company Digital* , as saying, "I switched back to my paper-based notebook system after a year of going all-digital. I prefer my paper system for a number of reasons. It gives me a break from staring at screens. It also causes me to stay in the moment and plan my days with intent. I feel satisfaction when I physically check an item off my list." Michael Grothaus did find it difficult to remember to bring his paper planner with him when he left for the office since he had built the habit of simply slipping his iPhone into his pocket. He also said he missed the audible reminder of an appointment 30 minutes in advance; but soon noticed that by physically writing down the appointment he seldom needed a reminder. I have written many articles indicating various advantages of a paper planner, such as the journaling aspect, the ability to review what you have accomplished in the past and the importance of being able to budget your time without overwhelming yourself with a list of

"To Do"s. But every time I did so, some people interpreted it as an attack on smartphones. Invariably I would receive comments listing all the things that smartphones can do that paper planners can't do – such as handling email and sending text messages and taking photographs. As one person said, "My smartphone will allow me to record audio messages, and set alarms. Let's see a paper planner do that!" To which I might reply, "I have a microwave that will boil water in 8 seconds; let's see a smartphone do that!" In other words, I'm not suggesting everyone should toss away their smartphone when they start using a paper planner any more than I suggest people throw away their kitchen sink when they purchase a dishwasher. They each have their uses.

**SOLUTION TO SHRINKING PLANNING TIMES**

A weakness of all planning calendars, whether hard copy or electronic, is that they allow you to schedule and list more work than you can possibly get done in a week. We probably all know that we should not attempt more than a day's work in any given day; because to do a so causes anxiety and stress and makes us more vulnerable to distractions and inattentiveness. And when you have more to do in a week than you can possibly get done, priorities frequently take a back seat to quantity as you attempt to get as many things done as possible. One solution to the problem would be to take one day at a time, listing only those priorities and urgent items that could reasonably be done in a day. However it is difficult to know what comprises a day's work. When determining a day's work, take into consideration the length of your working day, the interruptions that you anticipate, and the type of activities you will be involved in – and always allow up to 50% more time that you estimate your activities will take. *The Daily Priority Pad* helps you to limit to the essential priorities, important tasks and urgent activities to those that can be done in one day. This one-day-at-a-time approach allows greater focus, facilitates the changing priorities that occur during the week, helps you to quickly learn from experience what a day's work really is, and frees your mind from those items that need only be addressed at a later date. It can be used either in conjunction with or independent of an annual planner. When used with an annual planner with a week at a glance format, each page in the *Daily Priority Pad* is the day's action plan distilled from the broader weekly plan outlined in your planner. When used independently, normally by those individuals unable to realistically schedule activities as far as a week in advance, it replaces the annual planner. This short range planning tool is needed in today's working environment where the time between planning and action is becoming shorter each year, and in which the choices available to us are increasing exponentially. The *Daily Priority Pad* retains the priority and "to do" sections of the *Taylor Planner* , while limiting scheduled activities to a few appointments – either with others or yourself, and a "Notes" section for additional information or journaling. The *Daily Priority Pad* can be viewed and downloaded free at our website, taylorintime.com.

# ORGANIZING YOUR HOME

The logical place to start when you decide to limit the stuff in your home is at the source – shopping. If you have a broken water pipe, you don't start by mopping the floor, you turn off the water. In the same way, if you can resist those needless trips to the mall and garage sales and develop some good old-fashioned willpower, you will have less of a clutter problem. Your brain has a mind of its own. And since it gets a shot of the pleasure chemical, dopamine, every time it sights a shiny new thingamabob on the shelf, shopping can become addictive. And marketers who continue to get better at targeting our subconscious desires are not making it any easier. Buying and consuming will continue to escalate in the future. Get rid of a habit by replacing it with a better one. I feel you are able to replace the habit of marathon shopping with the activity of organizing. You can't be in two places at the same time, and when you're at home sorting and tossing things out, you can't be at the mall being exposed to the temptations created by the shiny new gadgets and endless paraphernalia. And you also get a shot of dopamine every time you accomplish a task such as cleaning out a kitchen drawer or donating something to the needy or gifting an unused item to a friend. You probably have no problem keeping digital files instead of reams of paperwork. It's just a small leap from storing paperwork as digital images to storing your stuff as digital photos. They don't need dusting, and in most cases are just as functional. If you miss actually looking at them, use the photos as rotating screen savers. But I think you'll find that out of sight, out of mind. Consider selling your stuff on Kijiji or eBay. An Australian survey conducted in August, 2008 by eBay indicated that the average household has about $3000 worth of unused or unwanted clutter around the house. The price of the items was determined by the average price of comparable items listed on eBay. I figured if it's true for Australians, it's probably true for the rest of us as well. If we held a garage sale we might be over $1000 richer and be able to move the car into the garage to boot. Just think; selling your clutter can become your bread-and-butter. If you think parting with your accumulated possessions would be too traumatic try this. Pack them into a carton or better still, a few transparent plastic storage containers, and stack them inside a closet or in the basement or stick them in your storage locker. Then you can easily retrieve them if you feel depressed or about to slip into a coma. But don't rent public storage. The eventual goal is to get rid of the stuff once you have realized you neither need it nor miss it. The more remote your place of storage, the more remote the chance that you ever will get rid of it. Most people don't enjoy their stuff even when it's visible. T he brain habituates to things that don't change, and you no longer notice it if it's always there. How would anyone have time to even look at everything, let alone enjoy it? So keep visible only those things you need or use regularly. And never keep what you can't use. I think you will actually feel unencumbered, free, and happier with your new uncluttered space and a sense of pride in your new accomplishment. You may also find you are more productive, more creative, and more able to focus on your significant goals and daily activities. Memorabilia that tie you to the past frequently keep you from fully enjoying the future. Recalling good times are never as enjoyable or as stimulating as creating new ones. Our brains are hardwired to be creative and to achieve goals. Clutter is to your brain as mud is to your feet. Don't let it get deeper and deeper and impede your progress through life. Be like the perfectionist bride who, when it was time to sweep down the aisle, literally swept down the aisle. A new broom sweeps clean and a clean start creates a path to a better life.

## THE FATE OF UNUSED STUFF

A survey on living spaces conducted by the magazine *Mindful*, and published in the June, 2016 issue, asked people where they put things they hadn't used in three years. Here are the results:

55% donated to charity.

22% let it petrify at the bottom of a closet somewhere. 6% chuck it immediately.

7% insist there's a use for everything.

Everyone else sells their stuff or puts it in storage

Of course, there are more creative ways of getting rid of it. Some people simply it at the curb outside their house and find it's claimed quickly by passers-by. Others have been known to even gift wrap it if it's something that they feel nobody would normally pick up. But avoid paying good money to put things in public storage that you are very likely to use anyway.

## PACKRATS LOSE TIME, MONEY AND SPACE

In this section I'm not talking to hard core hoarders who may need professional help, I'm talking to the bulk of us who simply have a tough time getting rid of stuff that we no longer need. And I use the term packrats affectionately because most of us find it a lot easier just to park something in an out-of-the-way place rather than get rid of it. Packrats are compulsive keepers. The things they keep are not necessarily useless but are seldom used. In fact, most of the items are squirreled away out of sight, nullifying any possible usefulness. Time, money and space are consumed needlessly by these superfluous possessions. What possesses these possessors to possess their possessions? There are many reasons, just as there are different types of packrats. One type of packrat not mentioned below is the collector. These specialists accumulate specific items, whether they are ceramic mice figurines, hockey cards or antique books. This could be classed as a hobby, and is not harmful in itself. Unfortunately it can lead to other collections such as buttons, beer cans and pennies, finally regressing to pieces of string, bottle caps and lint from the dryer. Collecting can become a compulsion in itself. Here are a few common characteristics of packrats in the form of an acronym spelling the word PACKRATS. A few words of explanation and a suggestion or two follow them. In general, packrats:

Put an unrealistic value on their old stuff.
Attempt to retain the past by retaining past treasures.
Comfort themselves with familiar possessions.
Keep for the sake of keeping (keepsakes).
Rarely part with gifts.
Always rationalize their decision to keep things.
Take pride in their possessions.
Seldom toss things out without prompting.

*P ut an unrealistic value on their old stuff.* Just because something was expensive to buy in the past, doesn't mean it's worth that much now. Most items depreciate rapidly and replacement costs frequently plummet. This is particularly true of electronic equipment. Items that we paid R 5000 for ten years ago can be purchased for less than R 1000 today.

*A ttempt to retain the past by retaining past treasures*. What's past is past. We can never relive it. Constant reminders of days gone by can prevent us from enjoying the present and anticipating the future. Getting on with life may require cutting ties to the past.

*C omfort themselves with familiar possessions.* It's natural to resist change; but it's not healthy. Old possessions that have lost their usefulness may not only comfort us but also serve to encourage the status quo. We should not seek comfort in *things* but in *people*.

*Keep for the sake of keeping (keepsakes)*. What enjoyment could we possibly get from things hidden in closets, stashed in crawl spaces and packed away in cartons? Out of sight, out of mind. We don't enjoy them because we don't even know we *have* them! This is where packrats get their name. If you haven't missed something in a year, get rid of it.

*Rarely part with gifts*. By receiving a gift you are not making a lifetime commitment. A gift simply conveys a message of goodwill, thanks, congratulations, friendship or love. Get rid of the impractical gifts and keep the message in your heart. That's what's important.

*Always rationalize their decision to keep things*. Ask a packrat why they keep something and they'll give you a good reason – one that's reasonable to *them*, that is. The favorite reason is, "It'll come in handy someday." It's hard to disprove *that* one. Packrats should keep in mind, however, that disorganization, clutter and space problems are a high price to pay for the off chance that the item may be useable in the future.

*Take pride in their possessions*. This is not true of all packrats, but includes those who believe that whoever dies with the most toys, wins the game of life. Some people measure their value by the value of their valuables. People in this category should base their self-esteem on who they are and not on what they have.

*Seldom toss things out without prompting*. Packrats are made, not born. They have developed these hording habits over the years. Firmly entrenched, these habits are hard to break. It's easier for packrats to change with the encouragement and reassurance of others. Giving them a book probably won't help;

they may not get around to reading it; they'll just keep it.

There may be little positive said about packrat tendencies. But if you have an elderly parent or friend who feels comfortable among familiar possessions from the past, it could be a blessing. Don't feel that you have to talk someone out of tossing away things that add stability and comfort to their life. There is a time to keep as well as a time to throw away.

## THE KEY TO GETTING RID OF CLUTTER IS TO START

If you were to only toss out, recycle, give away or trash one item each day, you would be well on your way to a clutter-free home. Clutter is anything that that you don't find pleasurable, meaningful or useful, and is characterized by too much stuff in too little space. To be useful it has to have been used. Otherwise, you may rationalize keeping something by thinking, "It may come in handy someday." Everything on this earth may come in handy someday. But it's likely you won't be around by then. To be meaningful, it must be some cherished heirloom or be attached to some pleasurable memory that brings joy to your life by its mere presence in your home. (Items bearing painful memories do not qualify.) It also could be pleasurable simply due to its beauty and how it enhances the space it occupies. Even so, you should ask yourself, could it be photographed, digitized, gifted to a relative or moved to another location and still retain this inherent benefit. If you plan to leave it to someone you love when you die, consider giving it to them now so you can both enjoy it. There are many ways to start. The easiest way might be to get rid of one item a day as mentioned above. In this case, while you are looking for one thing to part with, you will probably find several other items you can get rid of as well. If you feel you can dedicate a whole day or more to organizing your home, you might get four large cartons, mark them SELL, GIVE, TOSS, and RECYCLE and go to it. The cartons could be tailored to your preferred destination, such as "THRIFT SHOP, CHURCH, GARAGE SALE or AUNT SALLY.

# ORGANIZING YOUR HOME CAN BE FUN

## ORGANIZING TIPS FOR THE HOME

Here are 58 quick tips for saving time in the home. Check any that might be of interest.

1. Utilize space under beds by storing infrequently used items in low, long boxes on casters – or simply use cardboard boxes. (But if you never retrieve any of it within a year, consider getting rid of it.)

2. Keep similar types of foods in certain areas, such as all vegetables in the crisper, all cheeses on bottom section of a shelf etc. so it's easy to locate everything.

3. Twenty percent of your possessions get 80 percent of the use, so store those frequently used items where they're easy to reach. Stash the remaining 80 percent somewhere out of the way. This applies to files, clothes, tools, supplies and books, among other things.

4. Phone the doctor's office before leaving for your appointment to see whether he/ she is on schedule. You could probably utilize the waiting time more profitably at home or school.

5. Keep a TV or radio in the bathroom or kitchen to catch up on the news while preparing for the day ahead. Buy a radio that is safe for the bathroom.

6. Put a follow-up note in your planner each year as a reminder to change all the batteries in your clocks, TV and DVD remotes, travel alarms, flashlights etc.

7. Keep a record of family members' clothing sizes and a list of loaned items and other personal information in a section of your time planner.

8. To simplify bed making, pull up the sheets and covers before you get out of bed. This saves a lot of time running from one side of the bed to the other to get everything lined

up.

9. Before leaving to go to a store, phone to make sure they're open and have what you need.

10. Use plastic discs or safety pins to keep socks together through the washing and drying process. Or use a mesh bag that you can use for this purpose.

11. Throw out those part bottles of sprays, ointments and medicines that have expired or that you can no longer identify.

12. When cleaning out closets or storage rooms, label three cartons "Scrap", "Give away", and "Keep" for sorting as you go along.

13. Maintain a family message centre and a perpetual shopping list.

14. If you clip coupons, highlight the expiration dates.

15. Rinse the dishes and put them in the dishwasher directly from the table before the food dries.

16. Always have the season's clothes dry cleaned before you store them until next year.

17. Make the bed when you get up, tidy up the room before you leave it. The *do it now* habit saves time later!

18. Have laundry baskets for both light and dark clothes so you won't have to separate them later.

19. Keep a separate set of cleaning supplies in each bathroom to save steps

20. Set up TV trays next to the refrigerator when cleaning it so you can keep the items close by as you empty the refrigerator.

21. Make up a spare set of keys, everything from car key and house key to locker, office and cottage and leave them with a close friend – one you don't mind calling in the middle of the night.

22. For quick sorting of socks, underwear, bed sheets etc., assign each child a different colour for these items. For example, blue underwear for Johnnie, green for Billy, burgundy for Jimmie etc.

23. Keep several garbage bags at the bottom of your garbage can so you don't have to look for fresh bags when you take out the garbage.

24. Photograph bulky items that you have been keeping for nostalgic reasons only. If you haven't used something in over a year, consider getting rid of it.

25. Photocopy or photograph birth certificates, marriage certificates, passports, etc., and keep them in your files. You may also need to use the copies in an urgent situation.

26. Don't put letters, bills etc. back in the envelopes once you have read them. Keep them unfolded, staple the pages together, and place them in an action tray.

27. Near the front door, post a checklist of items to be taken to school the next day. E.g. Books, lunch bag, bus tickets, homework assignments etc. Encourage them to collect the items well before the mad rush out the door.

28. Switch from bedspreads to duvets to speed up bed making.

29. Label children's garments with an indelible marking pen to identify them at school – or in the laundry.

30. Use cup hooks or picture hangers to hang necklaces and chains at the side of the closet.

31. Keep a form to record loaned items (date, to whom loaned) and check them off when returned. Record borrowed items as well to avoid embarrassment later.

32. When storing infrequently used items number the cartons and keep index cards listing the items in the cartons.

33. To prevent having to dig through the linen closet to re-

trieve matching sheets and pillowcases, store the folded flat sheet, fitted sheet and pillowcase *inside* the second pillowcase.

34. If you have a habit of misplacing frequently used items such as eyeglasses or keys, establish a home base for each of them, and get in the habit of returning each item to its home base when not in use. For example, a key rack on the wall, a holder for eyeglasses on the coffee table, etc. It would also be a good idea to have spares of these items "just in case."

35. Have one junk drawer only. Use the other drawers to house specific items. Have a place for everything.

36. Set up a home filing system. Keep one file for income tax receipts and other files on major categories, such as Family, Bank Accounts, Investments, Legal, Repairs, etc.

37. Store empty clothes hangers to one side of the closet and use them as required. Don't let them mix with ones being used.

38. If you have a home with different keys for the front door, side door, storage shed etc. have a locksmith make them all uniform, then one key is all you need. (Not sure where I got this idea; but personally, I just colour code the keys.

39. Use a pocket shoe rack that hangs from a door to store small toys and dolls.

40. When you assign a drawer, shelf or other space for specific items whether it is light bulbs, socks or vitamins, don't introduce other items. A place for everything makes it easier to find things.

41. Exchange money for more time by farming out household chores, gardening, and home maintenance.

42. Prepare for the morning before you retire for the night by setting the breakfast table, selecting clothes to wear, packing your computer bag and so on.

43. When cleaning house, tackle those important, high-traf-

fic areas first.

44. When you wash the bed sheets, return them to the same bed, rather than wash, fold and put them away. You also give the bed a chance to air out.

45. Remove clothes from the dryer as soon as it stops and hang or fold them to prevent wrinkling. (If you forget, throw a damp towel into the dryer and turn it on for another five minutes.)

46. If you have different sized sheets, buy them in different colors or distinctive patterns for easy sorting.

47. Attach an extension cord to your vacuum cleaner so you don't have to continually change outlets.

48 Reducing double handling wherever possible. For example, putting dirty dishes directly into the dishwasher instead of stacking them in the sink, and putting groceries directly into the cupboards from the shopping bags instead of first putting them on the counter.

49. After dinner, set a timer for five minutes and have everyone in the house pick up and put away the day's accumulated clutter.

50. Make up checklists for recurring activities, such as vacation, trips to the cottage, etc., so nothing will be overlooked.

51. For your young children, buy shoes with Velcro snaps; they're faster and easier than tying laces.

52. Limit the number of toys the children can take out at any one time.

53. Teach children to put away their things, do their household chores, etc. by *showing* them.

54. Assign a filing cabinet drawer to each child so they can store school papers, personal drawings etc.

55. Reduce refrigerator surface clutter by laminating your children's favorite art projects and using them as place mats.

56. Reduce toy clutter by allowing your children to organize their own garage sale and using the money to buy newer and *fewer* things.

57. Bathe the children the night before so there's no bathroom congestion in the morning

58. Stagger bed times and getting-up times so everything isn't happening at once. Buy children their own alarm clock.

**GETTING AN EARLY START**

Bonnie McCullough, in her book, *Totally Organized,* says she makes her bed the moment she gets up, even before going to the bathroom. She claims she's not so tempted to go back to sleep, And no doubt that neatly made bed gives her a psychological lift and gets her on the way to a productive morning. Getting an early start isn't always easy. The bed is so comfortable and warm, and the alarm clock is viewed as an intruder to be silenced with a swipe of the hand. But if you can overcome that initial stage of inertia by forcing yourself to swing out of bed and onto your feet, the next time is easier. Soon it becomes a habit. Early risers tend to get more done; but only if they get to bed early enough to get adequate sleep. The early hours of the morning contain fewer interruptions. Telephones are silent. Children, depending on their ages, are either asleep or trying to compensate for those silent telephones. But if you are an "early person" and can function effectively at 6 a.m., you can easily get a jump on most people. A word of caution: getting up early and simply wasting this prime time on extra-long showers, third cups of coffee and yesterday's news does not make for good time management. Schedule at least one priority task to be accomplished each morning. Some people write books by simply writing at the kitchen table for an hour each morning. Others beat the traffic by going in to the office for a quiet hour each morning.

Others, whose family consists of "early persons", use this opportunity for quality time with the family. It can be productive time. But it's a choice. Will lingering in bed justify things left undone? And remember, procrastination is giving up what you want most for what you want at the moment. Having said this, getting up early usually requires getting to bed earlier. Never short-change your sleep in order to get more done. You will find that getting a good 7 hours or more sleep a night will increase your energy level, your productivity and your health.

# EVERYTHING I KNOW

**"Don't lose it."**

I apply this rule today by having a place for everything whenever possible. I store similar items together. For example, electronic devices, cables and accessories are stored in one desk drawer, writing materials, labels and business cards in another drawer, and so on. The key is to separate items that have some common association – whether it's how they're used, where they're used, or when they're used. I use transparent plastic containers instead of cartons so I can see the contents, label colored stacking trays for work in progress, and use organizer trays in some of the shallow drawers in my desk. You may need a junk drawer for miscellaneous one-of-a-kind items. The secret is not to let it expand into two or more junk drawers. When I receive cartons of goods from suppliers, I mark the contents on the face of the carton with a magic marker. When the contents are forms or other paperwork products, I tape a sample of the form on the side of the carton before storing it on the shelf. The few minutes spent doing these things at the time save hours when you need to retrieve them later. How else could my mother keep house, raise five boys, and hold down a part-time job.

**"Write it down."**

I never rely on my memory, even making notes while I'm talking on the telephone using a telephone log booklet that I designed for this purpose. In my planning calendar I record dates that I expect deliveries and assignments due, birthdays of family members and close friends, and things I plan to get done each day. I write thoughts on sticky notes applied to my laptop rather than interrupt myself when I'm working on a project at the time. One big advantage of using a paper planner is that you never lose sight of your past. You have a permanent record in your own unique handwriting – your dreams, goals, achievements, activities, and highlights of a lifetime. Your planners serve as journals or diaries – personal mementos of a flesh and blood unique individual, complete with likes, dislikes and personality quirks. You leave footprints long after you have passed on. You could record the same information in an electronic handheld device; but it's unlikely to happen. The purpose of the PDA is to get things done faster, not record them. At the end of each year, I print the year on the spine of my planner and store them in chronological order in my bookcase.

**"Put it away."**

It's always easier to leave things out rather than immediately put them away again. Frequency of use draws near to us things that are frequently used. People are reluctant to file or put away what they're going to need or use again soon. A messy desk results. Resist the temptation to leave something on your desk, and instead, develop the habit of putting things back where they belong after you have finished with them. Have a detailed filing system, adequately labelled so you are confident you can retrieve the item quickly if necessary. As we read more about the workings of our brain, we learn more about the importance of getting organized. For example, t he more items on your desk, the greater the demand on your attention. So keep your workplace clear.

**"Every day make your bed, brush your teeth and put out the garbage."**

What starts as a routine becomes a habit. And I seldom forget the repetitive important things because they become almost unconscious behaviors that I repeat automatically. Now I walk every morning, write every day and send tweets and post to a blog every week – in addition to making the bed, brushing my teeth and putting out the garbage. I recommend you develop routines for priority tasks that have to be done on a regular basis, the most important routine being to look at your planner every morning when you get up. This will remind you of the non-routine priority tasks that you have scheduled for that day as well as items on the "To Do" section of your planner. The above routine will help improve the planning function. Whenever you think of something that must be done, jot it in your planner on the day that you plan to do it. Whenever possible, that day should be in advance of the task's actual deadline. Make the transition from one day to the next both easier and more productive by developing a routine for closing each workday and starting the next. For example, start putting things away 15 minutes before quitting time, and set the next morning's priority task on the now-organized desk.

**"Get everything ready the night before."**

Planning ahead helps immensely in adult life. And the more organized you are, the easier it is to plan. Making a "To do" list is a form of planning; but not a very effective one. If you went a step further, and prioritized the list, and scheduled time for the high priority items in your planner, you would have a higher level of planning. Although a "To Do" list is a rudimentary form of planning, scheduling is planning expressing itself as action. . "To Do" lists are intentions; but scheduled blocks of time in your planner are commitments. Scheduled activities are three-dimensional; they not only tell you what you have to do, they also tell you when you are going to do them, and how long they are expected to take. And if something is scheduled, you know it's a priority. Things that are left on your "To Do" list are frequently postponed or die a natural death. Items that are scheduled as appointments with yourself, usually get done.

**"Do it now."**

If it's a distasteful task, but it has to be done, do it now and get it over with. Or as the oft quoted expression suggests, "If you have to swallow a frog, don't look at it too long." If it's a large, daunting task, you should work at it one chunk at a time until it is completed. Nothing is more unpleasant than starting a job that you know will take a long, long time. And time is one thing everyone is short of. But if you break the task into smaller chunks, each individual task is much shorter and not as intimidating.

To develop any habit, we must act out the new behavior we're trying to acquire – again and again. Repetition is the key. So the more you practice the "do it now" habit, the easier it will become to tackle large or unpleasant tasks.

# GAINING CONTROL

At the root of most stress is the feeling of being out of control. I'm sure you know the feeling if you have ever been stuck in traffic, or waiting in a long line or suddenly told that the unrealistic deadline on your project has suddenly become more unrealistic.

People have a natural inclination to control events and make things happen. Losing control makes them unhappy and stressed.

Here's an example. In a nursing home, the elderly residents were given a houseplant. Half of them were told they were to control the care and feeding of the plant while the other half were told that someone on staff would look after the plant. Within 6 months, 30% of the residents in the low control group had died, compared with only 15% of those who were in control. Another study had student volunteers visit nursing home residents on a regular basis. Some residents were allowed to decide when the student was to come in and how long he or she stayed. The others were not given that option. The student just popped in. After 2 months, residents with control were happier, healthier, more active, and taking fewer medications than those in the low control group.

Gaining control can have a positive impact on one's health and well-being. But when the researchers had finished their study and all visits stopped, there were more deaths among the high control group than the low control group, showing that losing control once you've had it can be worse than never having had control in the first place. This could be related to disorganized people whose houses or offices are in a shambles and yet are happier than organized people whose lives are disrupted by sudden changes in environment, workload, and interruptions that move them into a disorganized state. Those who don't rush through the day in a panic, but pace themselves and work efficiently, actually survive longer. These people usually have routines for going to bed and rising at the same times every day, exercise and eating. They control their work versus letting their work determine when they go home, go to bed or exercise. Mental clutter is just as stressful as physical clutter. Writing things down and having a plan to get them done unclutters your mind, relieves anxiety, eliminates the fear of forgetting and makes you feel better. We should never put our health at risk in order to gain more money. Otherwise, in later years we'll be spending even more money in an attempt to regain our health. Losing control affects health and productivity. S tress originates in a surrender of control. People who lose control of their time end up sacrificing exercise, regular medical checkups, leisure activities, relaxation, and healthy eating habits. *Keeping* well is easier and more time effective than *getting* well. Healthy activities such as exercise, relaxation and leisure time should be scheduled in your planner if necessary, along with your priorities and major activities and events. If you don't, the time in your planner may become filled with work-related activities and you may spiral out of control.

### PURPOSE BEATS PROFIT HANDS DOWN

It's important to have goals at any age. But it's also important to have the *right* goals. It's our nature to seek purpose. Monetary goals don't necessarily satisfy. And as people grow older, they seem to have less concern about profit. There is a study of *University of Rochester* grads who were asked about their life goals, and then were followed up early in their careers. Some had "profit" goals such as becoming wealthy or famous, and others had "purpose" goals, such as helping others improve their lives.

Those with purpose goals who felt they were being attained, reported higher levels of satisfaction and well-being than when in college, and lower levels of anxiety and depression. However those with profit goals reported levels of satisfaction and self-esteem that were no higher than when in college. They had reached their goals; but it didn't make them any happier. So attainment of profit or materialistic goals could have little if any impact on well-being. But it does impact the pocket book. Of course I see nothing wrong with having both profit goals and purpose goals at any age. But being is more important than having, and purpose is more important than profit.

**IT IS TIME TO DO WHAT YOU REALLY LOVE DOING**

Quickly jot down 10 things you love to do or would really love to be able to do. As an example, the first things that came to mind when I made my list was such things as writing, reading and speaking (which I already do to varying degrees) and learn to play the piano, and the guitar, and learn to speak Spanish (which I am unable to do and am spending little or no time even trying to do).

Next, quickly make a list of the things you are currently spending most of your time doing. If the two lists match, rejoice and take a bow. My second list contained such things as shopping (including garage sales), social media and Internet use, puttering around my apartment, and watching the ongoing political saga on CNN – all of which I could well do without.

I realize that we are all different people of different ages with different needs, wants and obligations. But we all have one thing in common; we are all getting older. Eventually we will all run out of time.

Delay is not the answer; change is. I am fortunate inasmuch

as watching less TV, spending less time on social media and less time puttering is relatively easy. If time spent on some of the things you are doing are not as easily reduced, such as housework, child or eldercare, over time work and so on, it's a little more challenging; but not impossible.

Downsizing your possessions and the size of the home that you maintain is a lot easier than downsizing your family. But you could enlist their help. A 2014 survey in which 82% of adults report doing regular chores as a kid; but only 28% required the same of their own children. I wonders why parents deprive them of their self-sufficiency. There are many ways of freeing up time from essential chores and obligations, such as outsourcing, involving other family members, taking advantage of government sponsored services or making changes to the way you are currently working. There are plenty of self-help books a good book that might motivate you to do this . You can't do it all. But don't let your current activities crowd out those things that you are truly passionate about. Personally, I am resolving right now to displace an hour or so of current activity each day with things I have always wanted to do and have been rationalizing that I don't have time for. Anyone want to join me? We can compare notes in the next newsletter. I have already bought the guitar and keyboard and signed up for Internet courses. Now I'm committed.

**TAKE CHARGE OF YOUR HEALTH**

You might think that neuroticism, frequently linked to depression and anxiety, would be considered a trait that would shorten your life span. But it could actually *lengthen* your lifespan, according to one study that was published in *Psychological Science* and reported in the November/December, 2017 issue of *Psychology Today*. Of the 321,000 people studied, those who rated themselves low on health tended to have a lower mortality rate. It's thought that people who scored high in neuroticism and rated their own health as poor or fair might make greater use of primary care and go to hospitals more often. This isn't suggesting that you become neurotic; but it could suggest that it pays to get regular checkups and not write off the medical profession simply because you have had some success with natural remedies – or nature itself . We also need the medical profession in order to live a long and fruitful life. I have been writing a lot about the importance of sunshine, attitude, lifestyle and environmental factors for healthy living. I do believe in the power of such things as nature, sleep, relationships, music and the environment to improve both your health and longevity. But I still go to the dentist when I have a toothache, and owe my life to doctors who nipped my cancer in the bud, performed surgeries when necessary, and diagnosed the diseases and complaints I have experienced along the way.

A staggering seven out of 10 deaths among peoples each year are from chronic diseases such as heart disease, cancer, stroke, dementia, kidney disease and diabetes. There is a plethora of information available in this high-tech age on how to stay healthy. And yet prevention is a hard sell – perhaps because we tend to live in the moment rather than prepare for the future. Preventable non-communicable diseases now account for more deaths worldwide than all the causes combined. If we took an active interest in our own health – enough at least to carve out a lifestyle that would pay off in the future – we would have a much better chance of extending our lifespan. We are so conditioned to "buy now and pay later" that we frequently do the same with our health – we overindulge or eat junk food and pay for it later in life. As far as preventative health measures are concerned, there is no "one fits all" regimen that we can adopt. For example, such things as acupuncture, aromatherapy and massage can be effective only for certain conditions and certain people. But there are some things we can all do that seem to help everyone, such as exercise, adequate sleep and exposure to nature.

## THE GREATEST TIME MANAGEMENT STRATEGY IS TO LIVE LONGER

I suppose whenever I pass another birthday, my thoughts return to my love of life. The good news, according to statistics, is that we're living longer. The bad news is that our bodies frequently outlast our minds. Dementia is on the increase. To gain time by living longer and healthier, we must look after our brain as well as our body. Physical exercise keeps the blood circulating throughout the brain where we need it most. It also helps to build new brain cells and improves learning and memory. So keep up a physically active lifestyle. Lifelong learning, and the constant mental stimulation that it provides, will offset some of the cognitive decline we experience with aging. Avoiding stress where possible, and being able to cope effectively with it when it does occur, will prevent brain cells from being killed. Minimize the hassles in your life. Social activities of any kind, where you are interacting with others, force you to practice cognitive activities as you carry on conversations. Diet can also help. For example, older people, who get omega-3 fatty acids by eating fish such as salmon and sardines, or take DHA and EPA supplements, are believed to be able to slow cognitive decline as well. An active lifestyle, both physically and mentally, is good for your overall health, including the health of your brain. And the most effective time management strategy I know is to live longer and healthier.

# PART 3: KEEP YOUR BALANCE

# BALANCE

Balance has its rewards. It reduces stress and provides greater intrinsic rewards, such as a sense of satisfaction and peace of mind. E xecutives who give equal weight to work and personal life feel more successful at work, are less stressed, and have an easier time managing the demands of both their work and personal lives. Balance is not the panacea and it cannot work miracles. But balance can help people sustain in the midst of stress and overload by keeping the highs and lows from swinging wildly. Thom and Art Rainer, in their book *Simple life* , described a survey they conducted of 1,077 individuals, most of who still had children living at home. The individuals were asked what they needed to happen in their lives for greater fulfilment. The majority of the answers revolved around simplicity and work balance, including time for the things in their lives that really mattered, and having better and closer relationships with others. Employers also benefit from having employees who are able to effectively balance the demands of work and their personal/family life. They have more motivated employees, reduced turnover, and improved staff morale, among other things.

**SIGNS THAT YOUR LIFE MAY BE GETTING OUT OF BALANCE**

Lives usually get out of balance over a period of time, either through poor working habits, a reluctance to say no, a lack of planning, lack of goals or personal policies, or a failure to prioritize. Signs could include such things as a lack of sufficient sleep, uncompleted tasks, skipped lunches, rushing, stress, missed family activities, and so on. A common sign is when work starts infringing on other areas of your life, such as family, friends, and recreation. For example, 58% of People admit that they skip lunch altogether if they're too busy.

Skipping lunch is an indicator of imbalance. Many people are too rushed in the morning to pause for breakfast. Skipping breakfast deprives your brain of the energy it needs to function at its best . Skipping breakfast is an indicator of imbalance. In our lifetime, the amount of sleep the average person gets has decreased from over 8 hours a day to 6.7 hours a day. Not getting sufficient sleep is a sign of imbalance. Total contact time between parents and children has dropped 40% during the last 25 years. A reduction in time with the family is an indicator of imbalance. Nearly half of full-time workers surveyed said they were too busy to take a vacation. Skipping *vacations* is an indicator of imbalance. The most obvious sign that your life is out of balance is the amount of time spent on work-related activities. Working overtime on a regular basis is an indicator of imbalance. Even in fast-moving, cut-throat industries, employers have twigged that one way to boost productivity and profits is to offer staff a better work-life balance. Electronics don't help in the fight to maintain balance in your life. They are not only sleep stealers, but they steal time away from other areas of your life . The problem continues to increase, the average smartphone user checks his or her device every six and a half minutes. That's about 150 times a day. One professional said when talking about his smart phone, "The reason I love it is that it gives me power. And the reason I hate it is that it has power over me." Work is no longer a place you go to, but a state of mind. And with iPhone, iPads phones and other portable handheld devices it's easier to be a workaholic these days.

# DON'T BECOME A WORKAHOLIC

## ARE YOU A WORKAHOLIC?

Answer yes or no to the following questions and then check your rating at the end of the questionnaire. If you're a workaholic, it's likely having a negative impact on your health and relationships. Try balancing your life by spending more time on family, friends, leisure time, non-competitive sports and hobbies. Cultivate interests other than your job.

1. Do you spend at least part of every weekend doing office work or answering work-related e-mail?
2. Do you take work with you when you go on a vacation?
3. Do you call the office within two hours of arriving at a vacation site?
4. Do you have closer friends at work than you have away from the office?
5. At social functions, does most of your conversation revolve around your work?
6. Do you do things yourself rather than delegate?
7. Do you resent having to take time off work to attend personal activities?
8. Do you feel your job comes first even when it conflicts with family events?
9. Do you always take your smartphone with you when you go on family outings and sporting events?
10. Are you more anxious to get to work in the morning than you are to get home at night?
11. Are you competitive and determined to win?
12. Do you feel uneasy or guilty if there's nothing to do?
13. Do you always read work-related material when dining alone, in waiting rooms and when traveling?
14. Do interruptions at work annoy you?
15. Do you create pressure situations with self-imposed

deadlines?

16. Do you get upset if things don't work out as expected?

17. Do you find it harder and harder to take long vacations?

18. Are you overly critical of yourself when you make a mistake?

15–18 Confirmed workaholic 10–14 Borderline workaholic 5–9 Workaholic tendencies 0–4 Nothing to worry about.

It is virtually impossible to balance your life if you are workaholic – so it is important to deal with this part of your life first.

## TRUE WORKAHOLICS ARE DECREASING IN NUMBER

It is encouraging to note that attitudes are changing and fewer people want to be labelled as a workaholics. Young people are not interested in working themselves to death climbing the corporate ladder. People want a balanced lifestyle and a rewarding life outside of work, with plenty of time for themselves and their families. Having said that, current work environments, email, portable digital devices such as smartphones and the lack of separation between work time and personal time all make it easier to work around the clock. It takes self-discipline, in addition to desire, in order to lead a balanced life. People are healthier, happier, more productive, and more invested in their work if they can separated from it periodically. Workaholism is not an ethic; it is a disease. You can still be ambitious, goal-oriented and productive without working 60 or more hours per week. In fact, the *Productivity and Quality Centre* once concluded from a survey that overtime is not worth the effort for managers. 85% of those polled said is not cost effective, since after 10 straight hours of work, fatigue sets in and productivity plummets. Working lunch hours makes the situation worse. It should be pointed out, that although we normally use the term workaholic as it relates to work, it can apply to other activities. Workaholism is not an addiction to one's job; it is an addiction to being busy. Compulsive busyness can take the form of hobbies, computers, shopping, housework or volunteer activities to name a few. Workaholism is not always physically unhealthy for the workaholic; but it certainly is for your family, friends and other social relationships.

**AVOID BURNOUT**

Keep your job and your life in perspective. With so much emphasis on success and achievement it sometimes becomes difficult to relax and enjoy life. Don't set your sights too high. Do the best you can, but don't kill yourself. Job burnout is a result of too much stress, and most jobs are stressful enough without adding your own unrealistic goals and expectations. Set goals that are realistic and realize that you can't do everything. Work on priorities – the 20% of the activities that will bring you 80% of the results. Always have some way of working off mental and emotional stress. Engage in a regular exercise program. Have interests other than your job. Make it a habit to talk over your problems with a close friend. And above all, remember that what you *are* is more important than what you *do* . It's possible that you work harder and faster under the pressure of unrealistic deadlines, but it is doubtful that you work better. Excellence does not come from tired harried people. Mediocrity does. You would not want your plane piloted by someone who had been flying for 12 hours steady, and you wouldn't feel too comfortable in a taxi if the driver had been driving all night. Tired workers cause accidents. The more time you spend working, the less time you have for other activities, including sleep. Even moderate sleep deprivation can cause brain impairment equivalent to driving drunk . Work smarter not harder. Concentrate on the goals you set for yourself. Every day do something to bring you closer to those goals. Recognize that you will have to ignore some of those unimportant activities that produce minimal results. You can't do everything and still keep your life in balance. Vacations should be blocked off in your calendar ahead of anything else. Relaxation is necessary in order to keep your mind alert, your body healthy, and your family together. Pausing to attend a funeral is not a time waster unless it's your own. Some people take better care of their office equipment than they do their own bodies. The human body is a lot more valuable than machinery. And with a little care and may have a longer life. But one thing it doesn't have is a warranty or money back guarantee. There are no returns or allowances. Spend all the time and money necessary for preventive maintenance. To prevent yourself from filling your planning calendar with only work-related activities, schedule blocks of leisure time. These outings with the children, that movie with your spouse, that tennis game or shopping trip. Schedule them in ink, not pencil; make them definite, not tentative. Most people schedule them with the idea that they will go through with it if something more important doesn't come up. And the "something more important" is usually job-related. Recognize that leisure time has value as well. Not in terms of measurable money; but in terms of long-term effectiveness, family accord and happiness, and physical health and mental alertness.

# MAINTAINING BALANCE IN YOUR LIFE

Maintaining balance involves gaining and maintaining control of your time and your life. This means that you should set goals in all the significant areas of life, simplify your life as much as feasible, schedule time for personal and family activities (as well as those other areas of importance to you) in addition to work-related activities. Life balance involves making wise choices. You might consider getting a different job that requires fewer hours and is less stressful or work part time. or you may consider changing careers completely. But these actions are a little severe, and frequently not practical – especially if you need your current level of income to survive. But simplification can reduce the income you need. I'll be discussing simplification later. It may not even be your job that consumes the bigger portion of your life. It could be other things such as housework, TV, social commitments or even golf. In general, people tend to take on too much, and sometimes they spend more time on an activity than is reasonable. To balance your life you have to examine your personal values. What is really important in your life? Build in the time for those things that are most important to you. It's important that you allocate your time properly. You could keep track of your daily activities for a few weeks to find out how much time you are spending on the different activities.

**DRAW UP A TIME BUDGET**

If one or more things consume a disproportionate amount of your time, then you can fix that by drawing up a personal time budget for yourself. Planning is important in order to avoid impulse spending of time. Plan what TV programs you will watch, the sporting events you will attend, the family outings, and jogging, quiet time and so on. That's what a planner is for. When I designed the *Taylor Planner* ( www.tay

lorintime.com ) I extended the planning hours to include from 7am to 10 pm, 7 days a week so that personal activities can be scheduled as well as business activities. Block off your vacations, evening classes, church activities, your child's little league games, those scheduled dates with your spouse, those special events, that annual cruise or camping trip. Sometimes you may have to schedule personal activities during work time and work activities during personal time. Balance is a blend of work and personal life; there's no guarantee that one won't intrude on the other – but it balances out. You should plan both your work priorities and your personal priorities at least a week in advance, and schedule them in your planner. Don't over schedule. I recommend that you schedule between 30% and 50% of your available time after work for the key areas of your life, including family, friends, exercise, household projects and so on. Allow time for last minute opportunities, family demands and spontaneity. You should have plenty of discretionary time. If you develop poor working habits, such as continually working overtime, working through lunch, not taking breaks, working at the kitchen table after dinner – your life can soon get out of balance.

**CONTROL THE TV SET**

The habit of eating in front of the TV set can cause problems as well, since we develop the habit of watching TV with no purpose in mind. According to *AC Neilson Co* ., the average person used to watch about 3 hours and 46 minutes of TV each day – that's more than 52 days of non-stop TV watching per year. And that was over a decade ago. A more recent report by *Neilson* in 2016 revealed that it had increased to 4.3 hours a day. The proliferation of smartphones, iPads and other portable digital devices have had no impact on the excessive use of a TV set. By 65 years old, most Americans have watched more than 10 years of television. Just imagine what we could accomplish if we could recover just half of that time! After work and sleep, television is the most time-consuming activity. So if you want to see the impact of not watching TV, take a one-week vacation from the TV set. You should really plan your TV viewing for the week, block out that time in your planner, and stick to your plan. This will avoid *impulse viewing*. You could always keep a record of the number of hours you watch TV during a typical week. You may not have a problem. Then again you may be surprised. It may motivate you enough to make some changes. One change might be to intentionally schedule activities with family and friends so they'll conflict with your normal TV viewing time. It's easier to resist when you have something else planned. I suspect I may be addicted to watching hockey games on TV so I sometimes intentionally schedule important events on the evening my Toronto team plays. I have found that it is not the end of the world if I miss a few games. A *Michigan State University* study showed that one child in three under the age of six would rather give up his daddy than his television. One of my sons and his wife solved that problem by getting rid of the TV set for several years while the kids were very young. Parents today have it more complicated with the popularity of the digital devices. Just as meetings consume a lot of time at work, TV consumes a lot of time at home. And just as we should have meeting-free days at work to concentrate on priority tasks, so we should have TV-free evenings at home to concentrate on quality time with the family. It makes sense to decide in advance which TV programs you will watch – then stick to your plan.

**OBTAINING QUALITY TIME WITH THE CHILDREN**

Be careful you are not enrolling your children in too many activities. They need enough involvement to keep them from getting bored, but too many will keep you racing from one event to another. Dr. Katherina Monassis, child psychiatrist at the *Hospital for Sick Children* in Toronto, says that overworked schedules are a contributing factor among her patients suffering from anxiety. She suggests that young schoolchildren are often better with just one outside activity. If you are a working parent and hard pressed to get quality time with your child, consider a family day together periodically, such as on the child's birthday, when you can take a day off school and work and spend the day at the park, zoo or some entertainment centre. Meal times are important for families so whenever possible, schedule yourself accordingly. In the *Toronto Star* , June 13, 2004, Barbara Carlson, president of the *Putting Family First* organization, was quoted as saying that evidence from teens is that they value parental contact most at four key times; early morning, after school, dinner time, and before bed.

### CONTROLLING ELECTRONIC GADGETS

Technology can make life balance more difficult; first, because of its addictive nature, and second, because of the way it has permeated our personal and family lives. I already mentioned that handheld electronic devices contribute to an out of balance life by consuming time and opening up more activities for us to get involved in. They also extend our working days since most people can't bring themselves to turning them off when the business day is over. There are advantages offered by technology but there are also disadvantages. More and more technology is eliminating the division between work and home. With handheld digital devices, we can be contacted at any time. Our *To Do* list travels with us wherever we go. So we have to be self-disciplined enough to ignore email and turn off our cell phones. A survey of 1,908 workers reported in an issue of Sam Geist's newsletter ( www.samgeist.com ), indicated that it is becoming difficult to even separate work from holidays. 51% of employees stayed in contact with work when they holidayed the previous summer. 80% of these employees left their cell phones on so they could be contacted by work. And 63% said they kept in daily contact. *Studies have shown we have more than 200 inputs a day – email, mail,* thoughts, decisions, memos, phone calls, and so on and on the list goes. But our short-term memory only holds seven items at a time. In June of 2008, the *Opinion Research Corporation* surveyed 640 workers at random and found that the number of Americans who work during their vacations had nearly doubled since the previous decade. And the laptop was replacing the cell phone as the most useful tool for working on holidays. ( *24 Hours news services* , July 26, 2008.) Although we have access to our electronic files whether we're at work or away through the cloud, we usually don't have ready access to our hardcopy files while on the road. And in some cases we may have to work in cramped quarters. Regardless of whether we are on a flexible hour system, or we're a telecommuter or a frequent flyer, the line between work and personal time has become blurred. We can work in the evening, in a car or at a ball park. As mentioned earlier, work is no longer a place but a state of mind.Boundaries that once dictated how we spend our time have become blurred or non-existent. Instead of three distinct segments of time – work, home and leisure – we have ended up with one large space filled with a mixture of work, home and leisure. You should stop thinking about work as a place you go to spend 8 or 9 hours a day, but as something you *do* . And much of it could be done anywhere. This makes it even more difficult – and more essential – to maintain balance in your life.

# JUGGLING CAREER, HOME AND FAMILY

## RUNNING A HOME-BASED BUSINESS

Some people are running a home-based business and have different challenges than those who commute to an office on a daily basis; but either way, you must adopt strategies that will keep your life in balance. These could involve delegating to family members, outsourcing some of the household tasks, enlisting the help of your spouse, streamlining procedures, eliminating unnecessary tasks, simplifying your life, organizing the home and office, being creative and taking shortcuts. Although the line between work and home life has blurred, we shouldn't let it disappear altogether. If you work from home, I think you should set regular business hours, complete with lunch hour and breaks. Business casual attire as opposed to pajamas and housecoat will help set a more businesslike tone. You should have a separate business telephone number so you can let your personal phone calls be picked up by voicemail. Make yourself unavailable to neighbors and friends during business hours.

## IT'S GOOD BUSINESS TO BE BUSINESS-LIKE

Entrepreneurs with home offices frequently make the mistake of answering the doorbell or home phone and go on non-business tangents. If you wouldn't be able to respond if you were at a business office elsewhere, then you shouldn't be able to respond if you're working at home. We teach people how to treat us by our actions. For example, if we always answer our phone during the dinner hour, we are telling people that the best time to reach us it at the dinner hour. And if we answer our home phone during business hours, friends will call us during business hours. By the same token, you should have a set quitting time, at which time you could change into more casual clothes, engage the voice mail on your business line, and assume your other role as parent, spouse or friend. One business writer claims that home offices are popular because they allow achievers to work endlessly while telling themselves that they are really spending all that time with their families. Family time does not simply mean being in the same room with your family. Working overtime, whether you work from home or not, is a bad habit to get into. It takes away the deadline and decreases your productivity. It also makes it more difficult to keep your life in balance. When you work from home, you have to build structure into your workday and develop self-discipline. Discipline involves doing what needs to be done rather than what we feel like doing at the time. If you have children, you also need help – whether that is in the form of a paid babysitter, a daycare center, or another family member depending on the circumstances. You can't be all things to all people at all times and still maintain balance in your life. I believe that those who work "overtime" on a regular basis are less efficient during the "core" period. We only exceed in extending our inefficiency to cover longer periods of time. I think we should be able to build a successful business using a reasonable amount of time. Life balance does not mean you walk away from the business at 5 PM every day. It simply means there is a balance between the time spent on the business and the time the other areas of your life. Delegation or outsourcing is one of the greatest time savers there is – both in the office and at home. If your charge-out rate is R 75 per hour, you wouldn't do jobs that you could outsource for R 20 per hour. Delegation or outsourcing frees time for more important tasks, allows you to plan more effectively, and relieves the stress of too many jobs, too many deadlines, and too little time.

**KEEP ORGANIZED**

60 percent of the stuff on most people's desks can be tossed. Sort through all the paperwork on your desk and either scrap it, delegate it, file it, complete it or schedule a time to do it later. Keep your desk as a work area, not a storage depot. Each piece of paper on your desk will distract you up to five times a day. Further, people spend an average of 22 minutes a day looking for things on or around the desk. And since most activity involves paperwork, the lost time due to a cluttered desk is phenomenal.

Treacy uses the example of a company employing 1000 office workers paying out $1,425,000 to people trying to locate paperwork. Regardless of the validity of the above figures, huge cost reductions could be realized if employees would (a) get rid of the backlog and (b) streamline their paper handling techniques and (c) develop the "do it now" habit when dealing with both electronic and hardcopy mail. This is assuming that all the paperwork is necessary. The starting point would be to question the need for generating, duplicating and distributing paperwork in the first place.

**HELPING OTHERS MANAGE THEIR TIME**

If you want to help your employees manage their time, here are a few suggestions:

1. Ensure that there are written procedures for all tasks within your department. Involve your employees in writing the procedures.

2. Insist that employees question everything they do. Is it necessary? Can it be eliminated, simplified, or combined with another task?

3. Let your employees participate in setting deadlines. It gains commitment and speeds up the completion of assignments.

4. Discourage unnecessary visits and shouting within the

office.

5. Eliminate unnecessary trips through the office. Ensure that everyone has their own 3-hole punch, stapler, pencil sharpener, and other frequently used equipment and supplies.

6. Hold brief stand-up meetings in the morning so everyone knows what is going on.

7. Periodically ask your employees how your habits waste their time, and take corrective action.

8. Set up a special time management suggestion box. Reward innovative short-cuts.

9. Provide training in time management concepts, techniques and methods.

10. Accept the fact that your employees need "quiet hours" as well. Don't interrupt them every five minutes. Let your questions and assignments accumulate and interrupt them only once.

Don't work up to the last minute and then rush from the office with your desk in a mess. Allow at least ten minutes at the end of each day to organize for the morning. Psychologists claim we enjoy our evening activities a lot more when we leave the office with an organized desk and a plan for the next day.

**MANAGE YOUR EMAIL**

Deadlines make us more efficient without losing effectiveness. So place a deadline on the time you spend reviewing your e-mail. With a deadline, you will delete more, respond to fewer messages, write shorter answers, delegate everything possible, and work faster. Since you may not complete all your e-mail in the limited amount of time allocated, you are also forced to prioritize. The ones that don't get answered are probably not that important anyway. So estimate the amount of time you are spending on e-mail now, cut that time in half, and schedule that shorter time period each day. You may want to spend half the allocated time in the morning and the other half in the afternoon. With some entrepreneurs receiving hundreds of e-mails each day, it is imperative that you don't let the time infringe on priority, goal-related tasks.

**YOUR FAMILY TOGETHER**

Hey dad, do you work past the end of the day?
Hey mom, does your job often take you away?
Is it hard for your family to be in one place?
Does Saturday morning always seem like a race?
Your schedule is jammed you're so busy with stuff
Quite often you'll find that you've just had enough.
You can stop all the stress, you can start to have fun
But do it together, for your family is one.
You can go for a walk, or a run, or a hike
Or off to a picnic, each on their own bike.
Then turn off your gadgets and gewgaws and phones
Just go to a lake and start skipping stones
Or prepare a fine feast, it shouldn't be rare
Enjoy all the stories, and don't leave your chair.
Don't answer the phone when you're eating a meal
No texting, no tweets, conversation is real,
And stop flipping channels and surfing and such.
Just turn off the TV, you're not missing much.
When you stay home at night to play a neat game
No matter who wins, you'll be glad that you came.
Your family comes first – or so you will say
Now make time for them, and do it each day.
The time you're together is always the best
So guard it with care and you'll feel truly blessed.

# SIMPLIFYING YOUR LIFE

It's difficult to balance your life when there are so many things to balance. Simplifying applies to activities, procedures, and possessions. You live on half of what you earn, and save the other half. That might be a little severe. You don't want to economize to the point that life is no longer enjoyable. But reducing your disposable income should limit your possessions, and saving for the future has to be a good suggestion, The point is to simplify your life as much as possible. The more stuff you own, the more time it demands. Most of us can get rid of half our possessions and never miss them. We could also rid ourselves of many of the activities in which we are involved and reduce the amount of time being spent on the remaining activities. Buy a bigger house and it may provide more space and comfort, but it also provides a larger mortgage, more taxes, a greater fear of robbery, more housework and more expenses. It does not necessarily make you happier. Just by keeping track of their spending, many people are able to cut costs by 20 percent by simply reducing any spending that is obviously a waste. If you spend your life earning money and you waste that money, you are wasting your life. Simplifying your personal life does *not* necessarily mean reducing your working hours, although for most people that seems to be an issue as well. It means freeing up more time and energy to pursue your personal goals and to work on activities that you enjoy.

**HOW TO SIMPLIFY YOUR LIFE**

The first step in simplifying your life is to decide what you really want out of life. What are your talents, skills and abilities? List your values, your friends, the activities you enjoy, what is it you want to accomplish. Then develop a set of goals, complete with time frames that reflect your values. Finally, de-clutter your life and free up time, space and money needed to accomplish these goals. It's really about aligning your life with your values. Some people spend more time on things they *don't* value. The more you simplify your life, the easier it is to regain balance. Your career may be consuming three quarters of your waking hours, for instance. Unless you're a person who lives to work as opposed to one who works to live, you might want to change that as discussed earlier. The important thing is to plan both your work priorities and your personal priorities well in advance. Otherwise one of them loses by default. What gets scheduled is usually what takes place. This doesn't mean there's no room for spontaneity. You don't schedule every hour of every day. If you have to fill in every space in your planner in order to get everything done, you're trying to do too much. Eliminate something or delegate something or both. Don't be an *Activity Packrat*. For everything you take on, get rid of something of lesser importance. Getting back in balance usually involves regaining control of your time by being proactive instead of reactive, scheduling time for yourself in your planner, simplifying your life, and developing good habits. It may even involve changing jobs, downsizing, moving or whatever. But it's a process, not an event, and could take months or even years. One suggestion, to align your life with your values, is to make a list of what's really important to you, and then make a list of the things you have to do the next day and compare the two. Most people have too many things on their To Do list. It's essential that we control our use of technological gadgets such as iPads, iPhones and and other handheld devices. They were originally supposed to give us more leisure time, but instead they simply make it easier for us to work all the time – regardless of where we are. Controlling them by turning those off at a set time each day, such as 6 PM, will help keep your life in balance. It will also reduce stress and help us to sleep easier if we're not checking email just before we go to bed. We try to get more done by cutting back on sleep when studies show that after a good night's sleep you get *more* done, with fewer mistakes, because of your increased ability to concentrate.

**DOES YOUR LIFE NEED SIMPLIFYING?**

If your life is not complicated, it obviously doesn't need to be simplified. When people simplify their lives, they re-evaluate how they spend their time. Below is an example of a list of possible things you might do to simplify your life. Modify it or add to it and check off those items that make sense to you.

1. Realize you have the right to say no. Recognize that every time you say yes to somebody else, you are saying no to yourself and are depriving yourself of those things that you want to accomplish.

2. Stop doing non-priority tasks. Delegate them, outsource them or eliminate them.

3. Limit the number of friends you socialize with on a regular basis. Have more family get-togethers.

4. Cancel your membership in associations that do little to further your career or personal development.

5. Get rid of unnecessary credit cards, consolidate debt where practicable, and set up a schedule to reduce personal debt to zero.

6. Build up reserves of space, time and money so that you can base career decisions on your goals and beliefs instead of immediate financial concerns.

7. Intentionally spend your time, money and energy on things that are important to you and not on every little thing that gets your attention.

8. De-clutter your home and office. Get rid of everything you haven't worn, used or referred to in over a year.

9. Introduce at least one timesaving strategy into your life each week, whether it is paying bills by automatic withdrawal, organizing the items in the medicine cabinet

or introducing technology to your workstation.

10. Cancel subscriptions to magazines, journals, newspapers and electronic publications that you seldom read.

11. Cut in half the time you spend watching TV. Choose the programs you want to watch. Never sit in front of the TV set with no objective in mind.

12. Keep track of your spending habits for at least one month. Stop buying things you don't need. Draw up a personal budget and stick to it.

13. Start scheduling personal activities into your planner, such as vacations, sporting events, recreational activities, physical fitness and movie nights.

14. Prioritize your *To Do* list and delegate the bottom half.

15. Don't save money if it means wasting time. Time is more valuable than money. Driving across town to get a bargain is no bargain. Similarly clipping coupons, washing your car etc.

16. Consume less. Repair items instead of buying new ones. Buy fewer upgrades.

17. Do less entertaining. Take more walks, hikes and time for yourself.

18. Drive less. Locate closer to work if necessary.

19. Cut your spending by at least 25 percent.

20. Each week ask yourself the question, "what can I do this week to simplify my life."

**SIMPLIFY YOUR POSSESSIONS AS WELL**

The more money you have to spend, the greater the degree

of fulfillment – up to a point. After fulfillment goes through the survival stage, comforts stage and luxuries stage, the curve levels off at the point marked "enough." As you start accumulating more luxuries after the "enough" stage, your degree of fulfillment starts decreasing. In other words, once you have achieved what the authors refer to as *enough*, acquiring *more* simply makes you unhappier. People spend their precious non-renewable resource, time, in order to acquire more money and possessions, only to discover that the possessions do little to further their enjoyment of life. In fact, possessions consume even more of this non-renewable resource. Not only does it take time to earn enough money to buy this stuff, it takes time to shop for it, learn how to operate it, maintain it in good working condition, repair it, upgrade it, insure it and use it. If we have to rent public storage, we have to sign a contract, pay rent, buy a lock, take trips back and forth to check on it or add to it, and so on. It's not surprising that the more we acquire beyond a certain point, the unhappier we get. We are afraid of losing it, breaking it or having it stolen. We frequently have to make payments on it, acquire more space to accommodate it, and worry about keeping the neighborhood kids or the family dog away from it. There also comes a time when we have to figure out how to get rid of it. The more stuff we have, the greater the responsibility we have and the more opportunity there is for worry, anxiety and stress. It also complicates our life, causes clutter and distracts us from our life purpose. This complexity can extend to our business as well. We can have too much inventory, too many receivables, too broad a range of products, too many styles, types, channels of distribution and so on. The years produce clutter and complexity that hinder goal achievement and profits. Simplification is a key strategy if you want to balance your life.

# SIMPLIFYING WHAT YOU DO

## A LIFE OF CHOICES

There are a lot of choices that we have to make on a daily basis. And this process tends to take time. But 80 percent of the problems we encounter aren't worth more than a few minutes of our time. We have to learn to say *yes* or *no*, *I will* or *I won't* quickly when the impact of the decision is minimal. Generally, you should delay until you have enough information but don't wait until you have *all* the information. Have the courage to make decisions with only 70 to 80 percent of the facts. Slow decision-making does waste time. Napoleon Hill once conducted a survey of successful people and found out that all of them were decisive. And people shouldn't be afraid of being wrong because we learn from our mistakes. The way people manage their time is determined by the choices they make on a daily basis. They can either say yes or no to starting a project, interrupting themselves, writing things down, or leaving something undone. They even have a choice of whether they get upset or remain calm. They choose the type of planners they use, the paperwork they keep, the books they read, the courses they take, and the friends they spend time with. They decide how to spend their weekends, their work time, their lunch time, their spare time, and their family time. One of the problems is the number of choices that we have; but the biggest problem is the actual choices that we make.

## SIMPLIFY YOUR TO DO LIST

Below is an exercise based on the priority grid; but it's a non-business example and we take away any reference to priorities and urgency and simply look at whether you really want it to be done or not and whether it *must* be done, such as paying taxes, or simply *should* be done, such as cleaning the windows. It's called the *To Do List Grid*. This might be a good exercise for someone who feels swamped and doesn't know where to start. It's really a process of simplifying your personal *To Do* list. We will never finish everything so let's be selective in what we do. We enter each day with the unrealistic expectation of completing everything on our *To Do List* and end each day discovering that the number of items requiring our attention has increased. There is never enough time. We sometimes feel as though we are walking up a *down* escalator, busy but not making much progress. As a result, we could become fatigued, stressed and resentful, with unfulfilled dreams, strained relationships, missed opportunities and a sinking feeling that we are losing control of our own lives. And the problem could be that we are not managing our *To Do* list properly. We are being swept away by its demands instead of taking control and making some hard decisions as to what should be done and what should be deleted. To help with this decision-making process, you might use a *To Do List Grid* such as the one shown below. The four quadrants of this grid are as follows.

**The "To Do List" Grid**

There is a big difference between things that *should* be done and things that *must* be done. For example, we should clean out the junk drawer, shop for a new car and have dinner with the Smiths. But what are the consequences of doing *none* of these things? Probably few. But if we ignored items such as taking a vacation with the family, exercising daily or repairing the stairs, the consequences could be disastrous. To use the *Grid* , you must distinguish between the *should do's* and the *must do's* and then separate them into ones you want to do and ones you don't want to do. You are the only one who can do this, because you know the circumstances and the importance of each in your own life, and you also know what you enjoy doing and what you don't like to do.

Let's assume that you place the following items in quadrant 1 as *must do's* and *want to do's*:

Make out a will

Shop for a gift

Take son to game

And in quadrant 2, those things you want to do and should be done: Organize your photos

Write an article Read a magazine

And in quadrant 3, those things you don't want to do, but must be done Shovel driveway

Walk in the morning Shop for new suit

And finally, in quadrant 4, those things you don't want to do but should be done: Clean out basement

Go to party Replace wallpaper

Quadrant 4 items are those that are not important and you don't want to do them anyway, so you might as well delete them. You have already reduced your *To Do* list by 25 percent. Quadrant 2 items could be deleted as well since they are not *must do* items; but since you would really like to do them, why not just delay them until you have completed Quadrant 1 and Quadrant 3 items? If they never get done, no big deal.

Since Quadrant 3 items are important but you don't like doing them, I suggest you do them first and get it over with. There is little fear of abandoning the Quadrant 1 items, since you enjoy doing them.

If you are going to gain control of your To Do List, you must be honest with yourself, question the consequences of leaving items undone, and concentrate on getting the important items done. Don't waste time on trivial things, and don't get sidetracked by items that are easy, pleasant and quickly done. If anything falls through the cracks, let it be those unimportant items. And don't feel guilty simply because things are left undone.

Must be done   Should be done

|  | Quadrant 1 | Quadrant 2 |
|---|---|---|
| Want to do it |  |  |
|  | Make out a will | Organize photos |
|  | Shop for a gift | Read magazine |
|  | Take son to game | Write article |

Don't want to do it.

| Quadrant 3 | Quadrant 4 |
|---|---|
| Shovel driveway | Clean out basement |
| Walk in the morning | Go to party |
| Shop for new suit | Replace wallpaper |

I really don't expect you to draw up a grid every day and divide your *To Do* list into four quadrants. But I hope that this exercise will help you to realize that you might be able to eliminate up to half the items on your *To Do* list if you are completely overwhelmed. And with little negative impact on your results.

It's unlikely that your *TO Do* list will divide evenly into four quadrants anyway. There could be very few items in Quadrant 4. On the other hand, *most* of the items might belong in Quadrant 4. Just because something is on your *To Do* list doesn't mean it has to be done.

### ELIMINATE LOW-VALUE ACTIVITIES

Simplification involves time or activities, possessions, and procedure. You will want to spend the time where the value is. You will want to reduce the number of possessions, which themselves consume time, and those things we choose to do should be done as simply and as efficiently as possible. The more complicated you make your life, the less time you will have to enjoy it. If nothing else, be on the lookout for low value activities in your life with a view to eliminating them. That will automatically free up time to spend on the high value activities that maximize your use of time and keep your life simple and uncluttered. In fact, I have a list of where to look for low value and high value activities. Let's review them quickly.

**Where to look for low-value activities:**
1. Things other people want you to do.
2. Things that have always been done this way.
3. Things you're not very good at doing.
4. Things you don't enjoy.
5. Things that always take longer than expected.

**Where to look for high-value activities**
1. Things that advance your goals.
2. Things you have always wanted to do.
3. Things that have an 80/20 relationship in results.
4. Things that you can easily get others to do.
5. Things that will conserve time, space and energy.

# THE ROLE OF MINDFULNESS IN LIFE BALANCE

You cannot achieve life balance without mindfulness. Mindfulness involves being in the moment mentally as well as physically. For example you could be at home or on a golf course and yet mentally be back at the office thinking about the project you are working on or worrying about the work piling up in your inbox. Likewise, you could be working on a project at the office and yet be concerned about something at home. In either case your body is be in one place and your mind in another. Mindfulness means living in the moment and awakening to experience. To enjoy your experience of being with your family or on a golf course or lounging on a beach, your mind must be centered on what you are doing at the time – not thinking about the past or worrying about the future. Our minds are frequently working in the future or the past: they seems to be its default settings. You can be mindful at any time, and dwell on the present as it happens. But it takes practice. Mindfulness is critical to the attainment of a balanced life. Mindfulness precludes multitasking, which is a bane to balance. It forces you to focus on whatever you are doing at the time. For example, if you are physically present with your spouse, you should not be mentally at work. Mindfulness improves your attention span and concentration – factors that are critical to resisting the lure of technologies and other interruptions in this digital age of speed. You could refer to the "gorilla test" described in the book, *The invisible gorilla* , where many of the students so intently watching players passing a ball back and forth, never even noticed a fake gorilla walking onto the court. Mindfulness has been proven to decrease stress and relieve the pressures of a busy day – factors also at odds with a balanced life. Stress has been associated with health problems, such as heart disease, diabetes and obesity. Because of this you might want to start with some mindfulness practices such as meditation. Or get organized first. You should find it easier to stay organized once you have purposefully set your direction in life and have learned to live with stress. There are many ways to develop mindfulness, including more formal meditation, yoga, and controlled breathing and relaxation exercises. But you can also practice on a daily basis simply by being "in the now" as you go about your activities both at and away from work. Using an example of driving or walking to work, you might try observing the street names, location of the various stores and service stations, and generally being aware of your surroundings. Be in the moment. Living in the moment, defined as mindfulness, is a state of active, open, intentional attention to the present. And it will move you from peak performance to peak experiences.

**DOING ONE THING AT A TIME**

You can't listen and plan your response at the same time. How many times have you been introduced to someone and didn't even hear the person's name? Try simply listening to other people when they are talking instead of multitasking. You do that by focusing on what they are saying, repeating information in your mind and concentrating on understanding what is being said. That's effective listening. Have you ever missed your turnoff when driving along a highway because you are thinking of something else at the time? You can't drive and daydream at the same time without consequences. You have to concentrate on your driving, reading the road signs, observing your surroundings, taking your dashboard readings, and looking ahead for your turnoff. When doing anything, a relaxed and alert state is the best.

That's when the brain processes best in the mind functions at its peak. The more you are able to focus on what you are doing at the time, the better you become at mindfulness. Research from the *University of California* showed that people tend to switch activities every three minutes during the course of a typical day, and it takes them even longer to get back to the original task. This leads to higher levels of stress, frustration, and time pressures. It's not a great way of going through life – preoccupied with thoughts of one thing or another and not remembering half of what you did. That's why it's so important for your body and your mind to be in the same place at the same time. Scientists claim that being in the *now* calms the mind and elevates brain function as well as reduces stress. When your mind is rapidly switching from one thought to another, your creativity is at a low. Some people are thinking of something else when they're eating and afterwards can't even recall what they had eaten or how much. Experts agree that simply being conscious of eating will help people eat more healthfully. Multitasking is conducive to neither mindfulness nor life balance. Nor is it an acceptable strategy for getting more done in the workplace.

**BENEFITS OF MINDFULNESS**

There are other benefits of mindfulness besides helping with life balance. An article in the special 2017 "Mindfulness" edition of *Time* magazine, mentions that according to 2013 research out of the *University of Pittsburgh and Carnegie Mellon University*, mindfulness practice can shrink the brain's jumpy fight or flight Centre, the amygdala. And the *American psychological Association* feels that mindfulness is also a hopeful strategy for alleviating depression, anxiety and pain. A 2011 *Toronto Globe and Mail* article reported that mindfulness practice was being introduced into schools to help children relax, focus their thoughts, and help them to function better. Research already shows that mindfulness therapy has potential for kids with attention deficit hyperactivity disorder and anxiety. Goldie Hawn, author of the book *10 mindful minutes*, reported that her foundation-funded research found mindfulness helped students achieve better reading scores, less absenteeism and a 63% rise in optimism.

### ORGANIZE YOUR MIND

It's more important to organize your mind than your desk or house. You can always walk away from your desk or house; but you can never walk away from your mind. We must first accept the fact that time is not life, as many of us in the past may have suggested; it is merely the medium through which life passes. And life, as you experience it, is not something that happens *to* you, but something that happens *because of* you. You create the life you will experience – good, bad or indifferent – by what you believe, how you think, and what you do. To create the life that you want, you must first organize your mind. And you do this by clearing it of all the worldly clutter that keeps it preoccupied and constantly distracted. One way of doing this is to engage in a 15 or 20-minute mind-clearing session each morning after you get up and are fully dressed. Don't do it while you are still in bed and half asleep. This is too important. It will determine how the rest of the day goes. And life takes place in a series of days. Complete your morning ritual of breakfast, getting the kids off to school, putting out the garbage or whatever your morning routine entails. Then sit comfortably in your favorite chair, and without trying to rid your mind of the random thoughts that will invariably invade it, do the following six things in succession.

1. Relax, close your eyes, breathe deeply, and just be aware of the miracle that is you.

2. Give thanks for all that you have and have had in the past. Don't rack your brain trying to think of everything – just those that come to mind quickly.

3. Forgive anyone who has hurt or offended you.

4. Offer up ten-second prayers, blessings or good wishes for at least three other people each day.

5. Think positive thoughts about all your future plans, opportunities and endeavors.

6. Decide and confirm how you will spend the next hour of your life. This may already be scheduled in your planner or you may choose something different.

Whether you call this session meditation, mindfulness, or "being in the now" is immaterial. What is important is that you continue to do it each day, modifying it as you go along, until it becomes your unique morning routine. And how you spend the next hour of each day will eventually create the life that you will lead. The reason for doing these six things will be explained in the next section.

**LET YOUR MIND CONTROL YOUR BRAIN**

Anger, aggression, irritation, frustration and disappointment are all emotions that interfere with enjoyment of the present and planning for the future. This clutter from the past can be swept away by focusing on the moment. When you clean house you are not concerned about where the dust, black marks and grime came from; you are focused on getting rid of them. When meditating, your mind is the broom that can sweep these corrosive emotions from your brain. What's past is past and cannot be changed; but you can build a new foundation for a happy, productive and self-fulfilling future. By being in the "now" you are releasing the past and beginning a new day. Giving thanks for all that you have today acknowledges your assets and resources, whether physical, emotional or spiritual, and provides a positive mindset. Forgiving others releases any hold they may have on you and frees your brain to follow your mind's directions. Your brain is the body's computer and it cannot be user-friendly while it is bogged down by malevolent viruses. Your mind is the organizer directing your morning meditation and determining the day's plans. You are not your brain; you are your mind. Each day is a new day, and how you spend the first hour will set the tone for the hours to follow. Start with your priorities. If your top priority is health, your first scheduled activity after a healthy breakfast might be a hearty walk. Or you might schedule a walk or other exercise later in the day. The important thing is to schedule the important things – those things that add meaning to your life and achievement to your goals. Actually getting them done is a function of the brain. And so is the attention that you give to each task and activity.

# PART 4: USE YOUR ENERGY TO FULL EFFECT

# IF ONLY IT WERE THIS SIMPLE...

### The Golden Rul e

Are you sure you're ready to stop procrastinating and to get more done, day in day out? All right then, here we go:

The best way to get more done is to **choose one thing** that you'll work on next. **Dedicate yourself to it entirely, without distractions or multitasking. Turn off ANYTHING that might bother you and keep going until it's done.**

That's how simple it is! So simple actually, it's nearly irresistible to sin against. There are always exceptions to the rule (like your office being on fire), but there aren't nearly as many as we permit ourselves. Every concession to this golden principle is like punching a **hole in a bucket**. Before you know it you're losing energy on all sides, and you can't seem to get anything done.

Of course, if it were that simple I wouldn't be giving you this course. There has to be more going on, or we would all be doing it – right?

# SELF MANAGEMENT

All Time Management courses and books eventually boil down to one central theme: that in the end, we ourselves are responsible for the use of our time. No-one else can give you more time, or take it away from you. *Time Management* is about the HOW: which **techniques and systems** can I use to free up as much time as possible? Techniques give us ways to work more efficiently, when we're willing and able to. But they don't resolve the issue of your colleague or boss walking into your office or swamping you in mails; or how to deal with days that you just can't focus. Basically, time management techniques and systems work when you have time and energy. Whenever those fail however, most systems fail as well. Just when you need them most! Because they take too much time and energy themselves, or they don't take into account your personal way of working and your blind spots that make you vulnerable to distraction. This approach is limited, because it doesn't take into account the inevitable patterns and habits that we have, that will clash with this new system or technique. Managing your time is about more than just calculating and re-ordering. It's about all of our unconscious motivations and fears.

**Building your own Time Management Style**

Because we're all different, one single approach can't possibly work for everyone. Certain techniques are useful for everyone, but fail because of personal reasons. If you want to learn to manage your time more efficiently and become more productive, you need to **know yourself and what works for you.**

This book will do just that: give you some insights into your specific time management personality and offer you options that you can turn into new habits and systems.

*Self Management* is about knowing yourself. What do I want to be doing? What are my **priorities and goals**? What do I do well and quickly, and what is difficult? Where do I lose time, what are my weak spots? It puts the responsibility for time with you and your choices.

**What type of Time Manager are you?**

The way you manage – or mismanage – time is connected to who you are as a person. Certain ways of organising oneself and ways of working are just closer to your nature than others. The **Social Styles Model**, explained below, can give you an insight into different types of people, and what drives them. The model also lists **your qualities as well as the challenges those qualities entail** when you exaggerate. Because every quality is in balance with its opposite: structure versus creativity, speed versus depth, people versus results.... When discovering yourself, you also discover where you are on each of these spectrums, and how you can enlarge your scope. The great thing is, working on this also means **working on yourself as a person** . The more developed and flexible you become within yourself, the easier it becomes to manage your time.

**The Social Styles Model**

The Social Styles Model is built around two axes, that create four quadrants.

**The horizontal axis is the spectrum Proactive – Reactive.**

Being **proactive** implies taking initiative. People that are proactive generally like speed and results. They don't need all the details to move ahead. Sometimes, they even move too quickly and run into walls.

Being **reactive** implies a more compliant and waiting attitude. Reactive profiles focus on depth and quality, more than on speed. That means they'll take more time for things, and let things come to them rather than go looking for them. Sometimes, that makes them on the slow or passive side.

**The vertical axis is the spectrum Relationships – Facts&Tasks.**

**Relationships** people value relationships above facts. They prefer to deal with the human side of things. They're good at making friends, forging bonds, networking. On the downside, they may neglect objective facts and lose out on results because of their emotional ties to people and situations.

**Facts&tasks** people want objective truth and facts. They analyse well and make their decisions based on rational conclusions. Work comes before play. These profiles tend to be more serious, and can come across as distant and sometimes even cold.

**Relationships + Proactivity:**
**The promotor sells him/herself to others**

Promotors are spontaneous, full of ideas, energetic, stimulating, creative, enthousiastic and future-oriented. You know them! They're the president of the sports club or personnel union and like to walk up front.

Promotors are **dominant and relationship-oriented** . They're real trend setters. They're interested in innovation, their image and reputation. They're original and like things to go fast. They also like comfort and luxury.

They can have **difficulties with** priorities, planning and maintenance. They also tend to stray on the superficial side, ignoring difficulties and tough situations. They like it if others are open, join in on their fantasies and illusions, and are optimistic towards the future.

| Time of your | Time Management = Self Man- |
|---|---|

| Life | agement | |
|---|---|---|
| | **Qualities** | **Challenges** |
| | Enthusiastic and dynamic | Tends to be egocentric |
| | Jovial and charming | Can be superficial |
| | Informal and loose | Impatient |
| | Full of ideas and initiative | Can't always keep promises |
| | Creative | Average listener |
| | Communicative | Not or badly organised, often too many appointments |
| | Sees needs of others | Rarely on time |
| | Motivates others | Plans little or overestimates him/herself |
| | Has good social contacts | Doesn't like routine |
| | Likes New and Exclusive | Has a hard time finalising projects |
| | Global thinker, holistic learner | |

**Time Management style**

Easily starts things but has a hard time finishing.
Tends to sweep over things and neglect details.
Not too reliable when it comes to deadlines.
Can get lost in dreams and future planning.
Has a hard time focusing on one thing for a long time.
**What you can work on if you're this type**
Learn to stay in one place, physically but also in a job.
Create structure in your life on all fronts.
Generate depth by staying and delving into the details.
Learn to appreciate 'boring work'.
Less planning & dreaming, more doing.
**Relationships + Reactivity:**
**The facilitator likes to blend in and get along with others**

Faciliators are **reactive and relationship-centered**. Examples of this style are employees that 'behave' and that like helping everyone with odds and ends even if it means leaving their work. It's the neighbour that always has time to help you out.

This type is more **accommodating** than the others, sometimes even docile. They want to have good relationships with their environment. They don't like being in the center of attention, but they do like helping others. They like to be **useful in the background**. They tend to **adapt**.

Because they're not task-oriented, but predominantly people-based, they'll often rely on **external guidance**. Facilitators aren't the once pulling the cart, and often they need a little push.

| Qualities | Challenges |
| --- | --- |
| Shows his/her emotions | Lets others take the initiative |

| | |
|---|---|
| Prefers to work in team – social and engaged | Tends to be doubtful |
| Follows the rules – loyal | Doesn't like too much responsibility |
| Is flexible | Avoids conflicts |
| Keeps promises | Will put relationships above tasks & facts |
| Consults others for decisions | Agrees with everybody to not hurt anyone |
| Takes other peoples' feelings into account | Puts others ahead of him/herself |
| Listens well – empathic | |
| Says 'yes' to make you feel good | |
| Glues the group together | |

**Time Management style**
Is flexible and helpful.
Tends to wait for work rather than look for it.
Works together well.
Has a hard time thinking ahead.
Will easily do things for others, leaving his own work.
Has a hard time saying 'NO', even if it's too much.
**What you can work on if you're this type**
Take more initiative
Say 'no'
Make your own planning and deadlines
Actively set goals and priorities

## Tasks&Facts + Proactivity:
## The director gives orders and follows those of others

The director is dominant and task-oriented. He or she is generally focused on the task at hand, and seeks **control and results**. Examples are the school director with a focus on procedures, output and control. The co-worker that controls or demands that certain rules be obeyed.

Directors are result-oriented, impatient, demanding, precise. They **don't adapt easily** to others. When they do, it'll be based on hard facts and measurable results. Don't try to pressure them, instead give them the feeling they can make their own choices.

They're generally **self-regulating**. They don't need much encouragement.

They can improve in listening skills, and **being open to other people's opinion**. They can also let go of solutions sometimes, especially where it concerns other people's problems.

| Qualities | Challenges |
| --- | --- |
| Direct and decisive | Tends to be inflexible |
| Defines clear objectives | Can be dominant and controlling |
| Well organised | Bad listener |
| Convincing | Impatient |
| Self-assured | The ends justify the means |

| | |
|---|---|
| Realistic | Doesn't like vagueness |
| No-nonsense – doesn't beat around the bush | Stubborn |
| Results and Action | Can be uncomfortable around emotions |
| Global | |

**Time Management style**
Goal- and Result-oriented
Organised
Easily gives orders
Takes initiative, makes things happen
Tries to do everything himself
Can be stubborn and rigid, difficult to work with
**What you can work on if you're this type**
Personal exchanges, working together
Don't try to solve everything yourself, ask for help
Take it easy on yourself, and others
**Tasks&Facts + Reactive:**
**The analyst observes, reflects and concludes**

People with an analytical style are **reactive and task-oriented** . This is the somewhat **isolated** co-worker that busies himself with **minute details** , poring over endless charts and complicated equations. The expert. Or the quiet colleague that likes to prepare everything perfectly and is always ready to research things.

Analysts are punctual, like to work step by step, are **methodical and detail oriented**. They work systematically, avoid risk and aren't satisfied with vague, global reactions. They're mostly **self-regulating** in their working style.

Because they're not dominant and task oriented, they're **prepared to follow the directions** of managers punctually.

Maybe even too punctually, as they may remind others of the procedure and demand the same punctuality from them.

Analysts have a **hard time making decisions**, as well as taking risks. They try to reduce stress by tackling complexity and problems that they sometimes get lost in.

| Qualities | Challenges |
|---|---|
| Rational, exact and precise | Loses him/herself in details sometimes |
| Organised | Has trouble keeping to deadlines |
| Prefers written communications | Not very expressive |
| Analyses before acting | Can come across as distant |
| Prefers to work alone | Doesn't make new contacts easily |
| Strives for correctness and quality | Is or seems wary |
| Problem-Solver | Often feels uncomfortable discussing feelings |
| Serious | |

**Time Management style**
Detailed and precise
Organised and analytical
Can be slow and stubborn
Waits for work to bit into, rather than creating his own priorities

**What you can work on if you're this type**
Set your own goals, deadlines and priorities
Make your own decisions
Work shorter and more globally, 80% is good enough
Think in terms of solution, don't lose yourself problems.
Exchange with others, don't try to do it all yourself

**What type are you?**

Of course, no-one is just one type. Instead, we have certain inclinations. You may be more of a director at work, especially when things become stressed, and more of a promoter at home where you feel at ease. We do have a center, from which we can expand in all directions. The more outspoken our character, the less access we have to other types.

If you want to be more specific, choose **one context** (the work floor, your relationship to your boss, family life, the sports club...).

Which personality and Time Management style do you have?

# PROCRASTINATION

Have you ever made (New Year's) resolutions? I bet you have! I'll also wager that most of those resolutions had something to do with your productivity at work. Mainly about how you can increase it, without actually having to work longer hours. Am I right? You want to beat procrastination.

**Reasons we procrastinate**

How many times have you begun your week full of good intentions, swearing you won't let yourself be distracted and that you'll get things done? Only to find that you're spending time on Facebook again, or checking your emails and not ticking off things on your list. How is that possible! You just want to get your work done and yet you keep on getting distracted. What little devils are at play here?

**1. We want instant gratification.** Having a nice nap in the couch may seem a lot more fun than going out running in the cold. Sipping on your coffee and staring out of the window is easier than working on that boring report. Checking your mail or Facebook gives you a quicker result than finishing the project that takes hours of work.

**2. We're afraid.** Maybe you're postponing your work because there's a problem or question that hasn't been solved yet. Maybe you're afraid you'll fail or look stupid. Sometimes it's easier to do something easy and save the real work for later. That way, you don't get confronted with possibly negative results.

**3. We get paralysed by perfectionism.** If you like things to be done really well it's probably going to take a lot of work. Just thinking about the work your project will take, you could easily get slightly stressed. In fact, it can make you so stressed that you never get started. You'd rather dream about the result than have to face the possibility of not having a great result.

**4. We're not children anymore.** When we were in school, there was a teacher breathing in our necks that chided us for not doing our work. In some work environments, the same applies. Under external pressure, however unpleasant, you do have the tendency to get work done. As an independent adult you're supposed to be doing this by yourself, which sadly many of us don't. You probably wouldn't be reading this if you did.

**5. We overestimate our future self.** We often postpone things because we think we'll get them done in some bright future where you're more productive than ever and work is effortless. Sadly, reality tends to be a bit more grim. If you're not working on it right now, in your bright future you'll be the same procrastinator you are today. Why would anything have changed? Stupid future self...

If you want to be more productive in future, you need to start working on it now. Every explanation or reason that leads to not working on it now, is just an excuse and will end up with no increase in productivity.

**6. We want to do too much.** We all know the phenomenon: you get so sick of procrastinating that you swear it's going to change this time. The first thing you do works, so you get hungry and try to fix everything at once. Soon, you're so swamped in things to do for the sake of time management that you're more stressed than before. Exhausted, you give up and fall back into the same old routine.

**Some starter tips to tackle procrastination**

*"All the flowers of all of the tomorrows are in the seeds of today."*
– Chinese saying

Becoming more productive is not a question of working more, but of being smarter about it. That often implies having less on your mind so you can work with clarity and focus. As with many things in life, your resistance to do certain things is between our ears. It's this resistance you want to deal with, before you begin with any practical techniques to do the actual work more efficiently.

I've tried pretty much everything, and these are the thoughts and things that work best for me. Any of these strategies can give you the momentum you need at a given time to break through your procrastination and get going.

**Insight**

Identify the reason why you're delaying. Discover why you're postponing the work. Reframe your resistance by discovering more about the work to be done. It's often our fear of the unknown that causes a paralyzing stress, the first step on the slippery slope towards that unproductive frustration. So map things out, create an oversight and insight into what needs to be done. Often, your fears will become considerably smaller.

**Make it small enough**

You can't get everything at once! Work in small pieces. Top athletes only think a few steps, strokes, or minutes ahead. For example, work in blocks of 15 tot 25 minutes (the Pomodoro system) with 5-minute breaks inbetween. Try to get a certain part of your work done in that block of time.

Install one new habit at a time. Plan time, prepare it, implement it thoroughly and do it until it's automatic. Make sure you have all the necessary means. Doing things halfway just gives you more work without the benefits.

**External pressure**

Tell others you'll be working differently from now on. Find someone who will check on the work you want to be doing. Make sure it's someone who wants the same as you (so maybe not your boss, that might push his or her own wants upon you) and who doesn't tend to give you any excuses.

**'Begin' instead of 'stop procrastinating'**

Your subconscious doesn't process negatives. What do you see when you tell yourself to stop procrastinating? You probably see yourself procrastinating, right? So every time you tell yourself to stop it, you're actually strengthening that image. Instead, focus on what you will do. What's the first thing you'll do? Take one small thing and start doing it, now.

**Begin at the beginning**

Often an end result we have in mind can seem so big it's overwhelming. Forget about having the overview, prioritising, planning... for a second. Let it go. Just do one small thing now, finish it and then do the next. Do that a couple of times, then collect everything into a big picture again. At least, now you're already created something to work with.

**Just do something!**

We often stop ourselves from starting because we think we're not ready yet. We don't know enough yet, still have to do all kinds of things first... But how often is that really true? What stops you is often less impressive from close by than it initially seems. When you think too much about something, it tends to become an incredible obstacle as all possible scenarios pop through your head. So stop thinking and make a first move, try some stuff out! Trust your instincts and improvisation. Often, the next steps flow automatically from just doing.

# IT'S ALL ABOUT ENERGY AND WILL POWER

Consider your energy and will power as if you're an **athlete in a long race.** To get to the finish in a good position if at all, you need to be very smart with your energy and resources. Too often we squander our energy on unimportant things: reading articles, watching videos, writing long emails, poring over details...

*You have a limited amount of energy and will power every day. Make it as much as possible and spend it wisely.*

To get things done, you need to use your will power. You need to select what to do next, get started, stay focused, deal with distraction, finish what you started, bite through the hard parts. All of these things take energy.

We often underestimate **the amount of will power we need throughout the day.** It's a general energy. You need it to get out of bed, to not smoke or eat that bar of chocolate, to concentrate on work or on the meeting, to convince someone of your point, to exercise after work...

One of the biggest reasons we can't stick to simple rules like 'Do one thing at a time until it's done', is because it takes will power we don't always have. **When we feel tired and weak, we let ourselves go and bad habits** – the easiest and most instantly gratifiying way to get through the day – **take over.**

That's why you need to learn to conserve your energy. And try not to do many things at the same time that take will power. Here's where your personal life creeps into work. If you're on a strict and difficult diet, you'll find other strenuous tasks become harder or make your diet harder.

Many things already ask for your attention and will power. This is your **Chronic Energy Demand**, like fixed monthly payments from your bank account.

*How much energy and will power do you already need to get through a normal day? What do you already pay attention to, try to change, restrict...?*

### Ways to build energy & will power
### Health

You've no doubt read this before: take care of yourself and you will have more energy. Just a quick overview of things to pay attention to:

Sleep
Good food
Exercise
Time off


### Feeling good about yourself

We have two brains: **the limbic system and the neocortex**. The limbic system, the old brain, takes care of bodily functions and feeling: breathing, emotions, hormone release, instinctive reactions... The neocortex is our thinking brain, that has structures and knowledge. When we get stressed, our limbic brain shuts down. That has a dramatic impact on our body and the neocortex. Our ability to think, to act, to feel becomes impaired. Being stressed is counterproductive. It's actually healthier to be happy with who you are and what you do, than it is to live healthily but feel miserable. **Succes & Confidence**. Every time you do something and it works, you become more confident. That frees up energy to take on new things. On the flipside, every time you fail you lose energy and confidence. That's why it's important to set motivating and realistic **goals**.

### Goals

Goals give us something to work for. Something to focus on. A reason to get up in the morning.

**What are you doing it for? What would you like to achieve?**

If you can answer these questions, your inner motivation will awaken and drive you forward.

Goal setting isn't only the essence of time management; it's the basis of a fulfilled and actively life. Goals give you hope and motivation for a brighter future. They propel you forwards and make you bridge difficult times. They remove the doubt and idleness and turn your life into a productive, happy one. That is, if you make a healthy habit of setting goals – the right kind of goals – and achieving them.

*SMART goal setting*

SMART goal setting brings structure and trackability into your goals and objectives. Instead of vague resolutions, SMART goal setting creates verifiable trajectories towards a certain objective, with clear milestones and an estimation of the goal's attainability. Every goal or objective, from intermediary step to overarching objective, can be made more or less S.M.A.R.T. and as such, brought closer to reality.

In corporate life, SMART goal setting is one of the most effective and widely used tools for achieving goals. Once you've charted to outlines of your project, it's time to set specific intermediary goals. With the SMART checklist, you can evaluate your objectives. SMART goal setting also creates transparency throughout the company. It clarifies the way goals came into existence, and the criteria their realisation will conform to.

*Why not think of a goal you want to set right now, personal or professional* . To make your goal S.M.A.R.T., it needs to conform to the following criteria: Specific, Measurable, Attainable, Relevant and Timely.

### *Specific*

What exactly do you want to achieve? The more specific your description, the bigger the chance you'll get exactly that. S.M.A.R.T. goal setting clarifies the difference between 'I want to be a millionaire' and 'I want to make €50.000 a month for the next ten years by creating a new software product'.

Questions you may ask yourself when setting your goals and objectives are:

What exactly do I want to achieve? Where?

How?

When?

With whom?

What are the conditions and limitations?

Why exactly do I want to reach this goal? What are possible alternative ways of achieving the same?

### *Measurable*

Measurable goals means that you identify exactly what it is you will see, hear and feel when you reach your goal. It means breaking your goal down into measurable elements. You'll need concrete evidence. Being happier is not evidence; not smoking anymore because you adhere to a healthy lifestyle where you eat vegetables twice a day and fat only once a week, is.

Measurable goals can go a long way in refining what exactly it is that you want, too. Defining the physical manifestations of your goal or objective makes it clearer, and easier to reach.

### *Acceptable*

Is your goal acceptable? That means investigating whether the goal is supported by your surroundings. You weigh the effort, time and other costs your goal will take against the profits and the other obligations and priorities you have with others.

Sometimes we set goals that counteract other people's goals. We then receive resistance. That can be unavoidable, like competing for a position. Or we want a job that doesn't fit with our family situation. Then the question arises: what is most important to you?

Some goals are be dangerous to yourself and others, like inventing a weapon of Doom, selling a terrible product at an exorbitant price or lying to make someone look bad and better yourself.

### *Realistic*

Is reaching your goal realistic to you? Do you actually want to run a multinational, be famous, have three children and a busy job? You decide for yourself whether you have the personality for it, or your team has the bandwidth.

If you don't have the time, money or talent to reach a certain goal you'll certainly fail and be miserable. There's nothing wrong with shooting for the stars; if you aim to make your department twice as efficient this year as it was last year with no extra labour involved, how bad is it when you only reach 1,8 times? Not too bad...

### *Timebound*

Time is money! Make a tentative plan of everything you do. Everybody knows that deadlines are what makes most people switch to action. So install deadlines and go after them.

Keep the timeline realistic and flexible, that way you can keep morale high. Being too stringent on the timely aspect of your goal setting can have the perverse effect of making the learning path of achieving your goals and objectives into a hellish race against time – which is most likely not how you

want to achieve anything.
### *My SMART Goal*
Specific




Measurable




Acceptable




Realistic




Timebound

*Goals in time*

Not only do you need to think about your Goals. You need to do it in different timeframes. If you set a goal for within four years, your chances of making it are way too small. You need short-term goals to keep you going, to give you focus.

And longer-term goals to keep you going in the general right direction. Both aspects are essential: working hard but in the wrong direction will get you nowhere. Nor will having wonderful long-term dreams but not working towards them right now.

Set one SMART goal for the same aspect of your life in each of these timeframes:

**This week**

**3 months**

**1 year**

3 years

**Build good habits**

Habits are things you do daily, on a near-automatic basis. They take less will power because they're ingrained in our system. They're paths carved out of the landscapes of our lives by repetition and determination.

Building habits takes time and effort. Another thing we underestimate. It's not because you got up early for one week, that your body will automatically do it the week after. In fact, many habits remain difficult. But most become a lot easier once you've done them for a certain amount of time. 30 days seems to be a good starting point.

It's also important that you don't miss repetitions. You can default one repetition once in a while, but never two. The day after should be extra strong.

Many people are swept away by the tides of Time. By not setting priorities and goals, or building the right habits, time and energy slip away from them and keep them from doing what they really want to. You already have habits, paths that you follow unconsciously. Some of those are very valuable, and others aren't.

Changing habits can be very challenging. It's like a rocket taking off from the Earth's gravity. At first, enormous amounts of energy are needed. As the rocket gathers speed and height, less and less energy is needed. Until it escapes into orbit, and runs out of itself.

Here are our tips:

-- Change small habits. Make it small enough to guarantee you'll do it. Small steps make up big ones in the end.

-- Change 1 habit at a time. It takes a lot of focus and dedication to change even the smallest thing permanently. Don't overestimate yourself, or you'll be wasting energy and creating frustration. That undermines your confidence.

-- Keep a new habit up for at least 30 days without interruption.

**Ways to conserve energy**
**From Multitasking to Mode-Tasking**

We've all heard that multi-tasking is bad. Even modern human begins can't do it without losing productivity. Automatic tasks can be done simultaneously, those that don't require conscious intervention. All the rest, however, isn't efficient. We are like processors in a computer. A task comes in and we run it through our machine. A machine works best if it does one thing at a time. Imagine a factory that constantly changes its production line to a new product; it would lose mountains of time. The same principle applies to multitasking: every time we switch to another activity, we lose time and energy on the switching process. To be as efficient and productive as possible, you want to switch tasks as little as possible. Similar tasks can be grouped in something I call **Modes**. A Mode denotes a certain kind of activity, a specific part of your brain processor that's being used. Being creative is a certain Mode that differs drastically from, say, copying a text by hand.

**A Mode gets deeper and more powerful the more uninterrupted time we spend on it.** The longer you spend in a certain Mode, the better it works and the more efficient you become. It not only takes time to switch between Modes, it also takes time to 'get into' a Mode. Like an engine warming up.

Years spent working in certain Modes, makes us **specialists** in this Mode. That's why the current way of scattered, multi-tasked working is no good: our attention span is becoming too short, and we never go deeply enough into any particular Mode to really deepen and grow its power.

Certain tasks can be said to lie **in the same Mode**: they're so similar that they draw from the same inner resources. Like calling people on the phone and talking to them in real life. Or physical exercise and repetitive tasks, strengthening our coordination skills. Or creating a new logo and a slogan to go with it.

Everyone has their favourite ways of working. Modes that they are **naturally more productive** in. It can be helpful to identify this and orientate your job towards it. It also helps for motivation: these are the jobs that give you energy and confidence. You can often start with those, and coast on that energy to start something in a Mode that's harder to you.

**Parameters**

Modes are often on either side of certain scales. What we enjoy, is the opposite of something that's hard for us. To find out in what general areas you excell, it can be useful to define some of your scales. Here are some examples

Detail work - Working on the big picture

Working by yourself, in silence - Working with people/in a lively environment Focus on tasks - Focus on people

-Creativity and Variety - Procedure and Routine

*Which Modes do you prefer in your work and life? Which don't you naturally like as much?*

Î *Which tasks do you have in work? Which Mode goes best with each one? At what times of day do certain Modes work best for you?*

Î *Create a plan to work in blocks according to a certain Mode*

Don't think too far ahead

It's good to look ahead and know where you're going. However, if you're always looking ahead you can't get stuck in now. Often, the enormity of what still lies ahead is paralysing.

When you think too much about things, it tends to paralyse you. There is an invisible frontier after which more thinking doesn't add to the eventual doing anymore; it's just turning around in circles. This is often coined as **Paralysis by Analysis**.

Many people struggle with this. They're trying to solve a problem before it's even there, or without know what the situation is exactly. Instead of investigating and trying things out, there looking at it from a distance where the hidden aspects of can't be discovered, or where the necessary change can't be started up. Examples are feedback conversations, project executions, forecasts...

Top athletes often only look ahead a few steps, strokes or minutes. Everyone can run for 15 minutes! That's why the Pomodoro System is so useful: you only have to focus and work hard for the next 25 minutes, after that you're off the hook. And so on.

Don't lose yourself in endless planning and trying to calculate how long something will take. Spend that time chipping away, that's the fastest way of getting it done and a sure way to not be disappointed.

**Finish what you started**

Don't leave open ends. Whatever you started, opens up a line that needs to be closed before the time and energy and invested in it can be regained. That includes promises; projects that are pending; conflicts that haven't been resolved; todo's in the back of your head; previous experiences with colleagues or projects...

To have a clear head, learn to close off the day or a task, and free yourself up for the next task. That's why breaks are so important, to give yourself the time to round it off.

Another part of this is celebrating when a big project is finished, and taking some time off before starting on the next one. Your body needs to process the end of the one before it can start on something new.

**Write things down**

Don't clutter your mind with things to remember. It's like juggling many balls at the same time, it takes too much energy and concentration. It's a chronic strain.

So write things down, in a place you can trust and refer to easily from anywhere. We'll look at my Master Daily Calendar System later on in this course, that'll give you 3 different kinds of lists you can access from anywhere. Those will be all you need to manage every to do you may have.

Another handy thing is to carry a notebook. That can be paper, like in the old days, or digital. These days, everyone who owns a smartphone has one with them. You can easily take notes and set reminders with your phone, and write short texts to keep your ideas with you. This is actually my recommendation. You can forget your Moleskine at home, but you probably won't forget your phone. That brings me to my next point:

**Integrate with existing habits**

New habits and systems work easiest if they integrate with your current way of working. Adding a small thing to your system is easy, and will pay of quickly. You don't always have to change everything to become more productive and efficient.

If you already have an online calendar, make sure you have it in your smartphone as well and that it synchronises every time you enter something new.

A great way to create an integrated workflow is the Cloud. Everything is stored online, and accessible from any internet connection. One of the best is Google, that has Documents, Calendar, Gmail and more. Pretty much everything you need to run an office and collaborate with others. Very handy.

**Find your time of day.** One of the most powerful integrations you can make, is to find out when your best times of day are. When can you focus best, when are you most alert and active? And conversely, when do you tend to be distracted?

Most people are at their sharpest between 07h00 and 13h00, between 18h00 and 20h00. That's when you should be doing the hard stuff! Other times can be used to do those 'filler tasks', things that don't really have great importance nor take too much effort, but that need to be done. Think reporting, preparing meetings, copy-pasting, printing things...

**Pimp your Smartphone.** Everyone has a Smartphone these days. You always have it with you, couldn't live without it... The perfect tool to help you out with your Time Management. Functions you can use your Smartphone for:

**Note pad** – Write down ideas to avoid forgetting. There's also EverNote, a free app, if you want something more elaborate.

**Timer** – Time how long you work cf. Pomodoro System **Calendar** – Integrate your to do-list with your calendar **Contacts** – Find your contacts instantly.

Aside from that, there are hundreds of possible applications you can add to your Smartphone. Keeping track of your budget, spreadsheet programs, daily exercise trackers... Depending on your activities and needs, turn your Smartphone into a useful tool.

### Eliminate distractions

Don't try to be stronger than your distractions. Relieve yourself of the constant strain of having to resist. Make as many of your unwanted habits unavailable. Turn off the internet or the email icon; delete your unproductive accounts and apps; find a space to work alone, or put on some earphones. Hide the chocolate.

You need all the energy and will power you have, so don't waste it on a constant struggle against your nature. Humankind will always tend towards quick and easy fixes that don't really solve the problem, don't fight that. Try to circumvent having to use your willpower by creating an environment that shuts of unnecessary distraction.

**Digital Distractionitis.** These days, we receive more and more information. We check our three email accounts on our phones, as well as our Facebook and Twitter. We follow a link to something else, and before we know it hours have passed.

This habit is no less than an **addiction**! If you want to reclaim your attention span and full productivity, you need to overcome the need to 'quickly' check things. There is no quickly. If you have to do it, do it well and within a **time limit**. Often we do this as a untimed break, which ends up taking more time than the actual work time.

*What can you do in your work space right now to eliminate distractions?*

### Pace yourself

You can't be a rock star every day. You have top days, and bad days. Nothing much to be done about it, however early you go to bed or healthily you eat. And yet we often expect the same performance from our best days, every day. We force ourselves to work harder, and create an exhaustion that eventually slows us down. That's not to say you should let it all hang when it's not really working, on the contrary. But you can be mild for yourself, and respect your limits. Adapt to the energy level you have.

The ideal dose is that where you get the best out of today, without using up tomorrow's energy. When we overdo it one day, we pay for it the next. It creates a yo-yo effect: one day you're up, the next you crash. Then you're up again, and so forth.

This isn't the most efficient movement, because every crash takes time to recuperate from. It stops the **momentum**. That's why it's better to stay lower, and in doing so avoid crashing. It gives you a more steady movement that eventually sees you getting further with less energy.

A good way to dose things is to compart your work into smaller pieces, like in the Pomodoro Technique. Create 25-minute goals, and create constant small successes. It'll make you more confident, motivated and productive.

Some activities also work better when you're relaxed. Everything that takes **precision, creativity and complex thinking** for example. You can't calculate by heart when you're in a hurry, nor dream up a slogan for your next campaign. Other things do go faster when you rush them, mostly **physical and repetitive tasks**. Think of walking up steps or stamping letters.

**Say 'NO'**

Managing time often means managing other people's time, as well. Some will offload their surplus onto you, pushing you into overload. Learning to say 'NO' can go a long way in helping you clear your desk from unwanted and unnecessary clutter.

A handy way to practice this is to try and say 'NO' once every day. It doesn't matter where, or how, just as long as you do it. You could decline a coffee, or an invitation, or leave a question unanswered. Feel what it's like, you might enjoy the freedom of it!

## Stop trying to be perfect

The urge for perfectionism is one of the biggest time-wasters around. Statistically, the relevance and usefulness of our time use decreases after a certain point. A good reference is the 80/20-rule. At 80%, most of your work is good enough. This first 80% often doesn't take that long to compile, create and/or streamline. It could be as little as 20% of your energy! The other 20% to get it just right, often takes ages and loads of fiddling around. This is called a digressive growth curve: after a certain amount of work, the added value becomes so small it's hardly worth pursuing. It could be that your job demands this kind of precision; in which case my recommendation would be to seek out systems to alleviate the inevitable but useless tinkering that takes up so much time. Create a template, a formula...

If you don't lose your job over it, I would suggest settling quicker. You're not doing your job better by obsessing over details, on the contrary: you're getting less done and slowing down progress.

Another aspect of this is that often, **other people's feedback** will bring you much more added value than your own process. Another viewpoint often adds that much-needed extra. So stop earlier and show it to others for feedback quicker. That way, you'll also avoid double work that you did based on assumptions that turned out to be wrong.

**Be mild for yourself. 80% is often not only good enough, it's also very efficient!**

## Don't do everything yourself

Not only is this tiring, it's also inefficient. Unless you're Superman, chances are certain parts of your work are better done by others. Or maybe they need more time and deliver less quality, and still it's a good idea to let them do it.

Why? Because you may be able to use your time for more valuable tasks. If you're the business owner or manager, you need to be managing the overall picture. If you don't do that, the whole department or company will suffer. The people you hire are there to take care of the details. As you'll also see in the part about Modes, certain people are better at certain tasks than others. If you can delegate the tasks to the right person in your team and possibly take on some of their work that you're better at, your group team becomes significantly more efficient.

*Who in your team is better at certain tasks?*
*What are your own specialties?*
*What could you give to others, and take over from others?*

### More Ways to Improve Productivity

With a few small changes, you can set a chain in motion to get more done in less time. Here are ten possible changes you can make to achieve just that:

**1. Work on your future self – today.** Unless you do something about it in the meantime, you'll procrastinate as much later as you do today. It's like that movie, 'Back to the Future' – it's up to you now, in the past of your future, to influence how your future self will tackle his present (you have to love that sentence). That doesn't mean you should become the most productive person in one day, but you can make an ongoing commitment out of it. Keep working on it, and before you know it you'll have created it a brighter future for yourself.

**2. Be productive, even when you're not working.** Maintain a list with small productive tasks you can do as a break. Cleaning (parts) of your desk(top), calling a customer, looking something up for your next holiday... Things that need to be done and that take no more than five minutes. This kind of thing clears your head, gives you a breather and gets you ready for the next big task.

3. **Get up earlier**. Are you one of those people (like me) who get up just in time to shower, grab some grub on the go and rush off the work? Why not get up half an hour earlier! Ban the snooze button. It doesn't make you any more slept out, and your day can begin with a lot less stress. You could even meditate before work!

4. **Prepare your day**. If getting up earlier isn't your cup of tea, how about taking time at the end of each day to create some peace of mind for tomorrow morning? Plan your work, put things ready so you can jump right in. That way you don't need to wake up with that slight feeling of panicky dread at the unpredictability of today's tasks: you already know what's going to happen.

5. **Put a limit on your time**. It's ironic: so many people work long hours and think they're doing great. Sadly, the amount of hours spent working are no reference to getting things done. Your mind works better and faster when it has constraints. An impending deadline makes you many times more productive. So harness the power of time: limit the amount of hours you work and work more productively while you're at it.

6. **Limit your to do-list**. We often have the tendency to put too many things on the list, and then hop from one job to the other, just getting small parts of each done and generally losing loads of time getting into each task. So make that long, complete list... and then select the 3 to 5 things that you really want to get done. Make sure that when you get these done, you can be satisfied about your day. Start with the most im-

portant, before you do anything else (especially before checking your email).

**7. Apply the principle of TV commercials**. Some TV channels begin with a new programme as soon as the previous one finishes. A few minutes later, in come commercials. Why? Because by then, people are already watching the next programme. They want to see what happens. The same goes for your work: don't take breaks in between tasks, but a little while after you've begun a new task. That way you also have concrete things to think about, and you'll automatically start working sooner.

**8. Force yourself to take short breaks**. Everyone deserves a treat after working hard. But don't break too long! A few minutes to catch your breath is more than enough, rather than losing your momentum with a half-hour break.

**9. Fix a time for recreation**. Social networks like Facebook are a powerful way to stay connected, but two or three times a day for five minutes should suffice. After that it becomes a waste of time, like many other online and offline recreations. Fix a time for them, like from five to five thirty.

**10. Minimise work-home travel**. You can't always choose where you work. But you can find the most productive way to get there. You can carpool, or take public transportation. That gives you the chance to not have to drive, which is basically a waste of valuable time. Spend it reviewing your day, preparing something, reading up on important news... This time is often well used for long-term things.

**11. Stop reading about time management**. There's a big difference between knowing something and being able to do something. You probably already know everything you need, especially if you know the Golden Rule of Productivity. It's like knowing how a car works, but not being able to fix it yourself. So take one practical thing and do it until it's a habit.

**EXTRA – What's the best work music?**

If you like listening to music while you work, consider the following points to decide whether or not it's helping you to focus or not. Here are some points that define whether or not music is helping you, or distracting you.

To start with, to concentrate you need music **without words**. Even if you're not listening, talking takes up part of your attention. Ever notice how a certain word or line from a song makes you prick up your ears? How can you hear that word if you're not listening at all... Music needs to support your attention, not take away from it.

A good bet is **computer game music**. It's not exactly Music Awards material, but it is specifically designed for you to do better at the game. That implies not being distracted by it, and helping you perform arduous concentration tasks. It puts you in a **concentrated trance**.

Jazz is often used but actually isn't the best music, it contains too many unexpected turns and twists. This can also be the case with classical music. You're looking for **music that's slightly repetitive without becoming annoying**.

Also think of the right **rhythm**. Techno = 120–150 bpm = fast, allegro moderato = 80 bpm relaxed. Some jobs need up-tempo, for other tasks you need to be very calm. Your guide to classical music rhythms, from slower to faster:

- Larghissimo – very, very slow (19 BPM and under)

- Grave – slow and solemn (20–40 BPM)

- Lento – slowly (40–45 BPM)

- Largo – broadly (45–50 BPM)

- Larghetto – rather broadly (50–55 BPM)

- Adagio – slow and stately (literally, "at ease") (55–65 BPM)

- Adagietto – rather slow (65–69 BPM)

- Andante moderato – a bit slower than andante (69–72 BPM)

- Andante – at a walking pace (73–77 BPM)

- Andantino – slightly faster than andante (although in some cases it can be taken to mean slightly slower than andante) (78–83 BPM)

- Marcia moderato – moderately, in the manner of a march [4][5] (83–85 BPM)

- Moderato – moderately (86–97 BPM)

- Allegretto – moderately fast (98–109 BPM)

- Allegro – fast, quickly, and bright (109–132 BPM)

- Vivace – lively and fast (132–140 BPM)

- Vivacissimo – very fast and lively (140–150 BPM)

- Allegrissimo – very fast (150–167 BPM)

- Presto – extremely fast (168–177 BPM)

- Prestissimo – even faster than Presto (178 BPM and over)

# HOW TO SET PRIORITIES

What often goes wrong in our work is that we allow unimportant tasks to take precedence over more essential things. Because they're faster, easier, more urgent. That way, we end up in a rut of endless operational tasks that never allows us the time to work on those dream projects of ours. What to do?

It's all about importance:

Doing something unimportant well doesn't make it more important.

Needing a lot of time doesn't make it more important.

We run around saying: 'If only I had more time, I could get everything done.' The good news is: you do! The bad news: you'll have to let some things go. If you don't, more time would just give you more meaningless tasks to fill it up with. What you need is to stay conscient of and focused on what's really important. That's the only way to get the big things done in life!

**Time Management Grid**

I've been using this to create clarity in my todo's for ages, which has completely changed my view on my work. I used to be stressed all the time and complain about not being able to do what I wanted; now I just decide what I want to do and make time for it. So let's get to it! Take at the quadrant below and put it on a big piece of paper, but keep the squares empty. Now what are these quadrants all about?

**Sector I: Urgent and Important**
Crises
Urgent problems
Deadlines from above
**Sector II: Not Urgent but Important**
Prevention and Planning

Relationship building
Business and Personal Development
Long Term Goals

**Sector III: Urgent but not Important**
Interruptions: mails, calls, reports, meetings...
Other people's problems

**Sector IV: Nor Urgent Nor Important**
Trivia, entertainment
Things that might become important one day
Distraction (Facebook, the window)

Things in Sector I are both Urgent and Important. These are most often things that come from others: deadlines for clients, reports for you manager... Things that need to be done yesterday, or things will blow up. Sector II contains things that are important, but not urgent. It's our real goals, the things we want to realize in life. Sadly, it's also the things that we delay because of things in Sector I – or worse, in Sector III: things that are urgent but not important at all.

A good planning creates a balance between sectors I and II. Ideally, you should clear out Sector I completely and work only in Sector II. As for Sectors III en IV: it may sound harsh, but I think it's best you let them go. Especially as long as there are still things to do in Sector I or II.

**Tip: put deadlines on Sector II**

The things in Sector II are often what makes us tick and love our work. And yet, often we can't seem to get them done. One of the main reasons is often no-one will blame or fire you if you don't do them.

You can add extra pressure for yourself though, by setting deadlines. You're slowly bringing them into Sector I, and increasing the pressure to realise them. Don't forget: the most important appointment you have is the one with yourself!

**Tip: Are your priorities your own?**

Other people would dare to 'delegate' their problems and tasks to us. By making them seem urgent and important, they're dropped into your Sector I. Don't let them fool you! You may recognise these sentences: "It'll only take a minute"; "Who else is going to do it?!"; "It simply has to be done by tomorrow or..."; "They told me you had to do it NOW."...

Often those things aren't all that important or urgent at all. You find you've set your work aside, made things happen and two weeks later, you still haven't heard back about it. Learning to sidestep or delegate these things back can be a handy skill. Here are some useful lines:

I'll do it right after I finish this important assignment!

Sorry, I'm fully booked until tomorrow evening. Things that are even more pressing than this. Who exactly said it needed to be finished?

I'd love to do it. I'll need XXX first though, can you send it to me and then I'll start on it.

**How to decide what's important (or not)**

If you find you have nothing to put in Sector III and IV, you're probably taking on too much. Choose what you really want to get done, and what you could live without. Let them go for the time being. Focus on those things that are essential to you, and forget about all the rest. Result: more focus, less clutter!

*Assignment* : fill in all of your work, projects, dreams... in these quadrants. Take a look at your planning and work: are they in concordance with your priorities? If not, adapt your planning!

Let's make it even more interesting...

**Imagine that, for some reason, you can only work for 2 hours a day. Which tasks would you choose. What would**

you drop?

  Now imagine you only have 2 hours a week. Which tasks would you do? Which would you drop?

# SYSTEMS IN SHORT

**Master Daily Calendar system**

This is my super-simple way of keeping track of things. As most systems take a lot of time and effort to set up and run, they tend to only work in easy times. When things get stressed, maintenance of the system suffers and we run behind our schedules.

It takes three lists:

**Your 'Master' List.** This is where you throw in everything that needs to be done. I recommend using the two first quadrants. That gives you a quick overview of what needs to be done in the near future, and what you want to work on long-term.

Throw everything in here, possibly including some more info and dates. But keep it short! Don't worry about ordering it, that work again. You could of course do it in Excel, and add a deadline for each thing that allows you to quickly order it with Excel's Order function.

**Your 'Today' List.** This is what you want to have done today. It contains 5 items at most! Make sure this list feels **feasible and light**. Our work tends to make things heavier in itself, no need to overload yourself in advance. For me, 3 solid tasks a day are perfect.

**Your Calendar.** There are always things you need to plan out in advance, or blocks of time you want to reserve for a particular task. I personally put these in my **Google calendar** (if you use OutLook, just as good).

It contains both my personal and professional appointments, as well as blocks of time set aside for certain tasks. In that way, I can run my to do-lists and my calendar side by side, with a minimum of hassle. What's more, I can assess the real workload of a certain period of time because everything is in there, from my dinner dates to reserved time for preparing a presentation.

That's it. It's very simple and it takes up little to no time to make and maintain. Integrating it into your calendar means you're just adding onto something you're already using. Don't spend too much time planning: often, it's an excuse to not be working on things.

**My System**

**My System** ' basic time management system is built on the mindset that time management should be simple and uncomplicated. He recounts a time management seminar he attended where the speaker told them to track how they use their time for three months. He couldn't believe his ears! He just rolled his eyes, gathered his things and left the seminar. He went on to devise a simple time management system that he could use in managing his businesses.

Here is the essence of it:

1. Touch it once.
2. Make lists.
3. Plan how much time you will allocate to each task.
4. Plan the day.
5. Prioritize.
6. Ask yourself: "Will it hurt me to throw this away?"

**1. Touch it once.** Do not begin a task if you aren't ready to deal with it. A concrete example is email. Once you open and read your emails, prepare to do the action items you find right there and then. With the prevalence of emails in our communication, we tend to just read the email, try to remember what it said and decide to go back to it later in the day.

That is a waste of time! If you could just allot 3–5 minutes to do what is asked by the email, you can discard that email right away and then move on with your other tasks. The lesson here is simple: once you touch it, deal with it!

**2. Make lists.** Lists are a great way to organize your tasks for the day, for the week, and for the month. You can prepare as many lists as you can, store them on your planner or your computer. Be careful though. If you list down too many things, you will end up not finishing them all by the end of the day. That will also have a negative psychological effect on you. You may feel as if you're doing everything you can and still it is not enough. Or that you may end up feeling that lists are nonsense!

I suggests listing down only 6 items that you must absolutely do for the day. No more. No less. This way, you could look back at the day and be satisfied that you have done your best.

**3. Plan how much time you will allocate to each task.** After creating a list, you need to estimate the number of hours (or minutes, perhaps) you need to allocate for each task. Ideally, each task should only take you up to an hour. Six tasks would then be done within 6 hours. That leaves you with extra time for checking your emails, going to meetings and other routine tasks in your office. If the number of hours exceeds ten hours, then perhaps, you need to reassess your work habits. Perhaps, you are not working as efficiently as possible!

**4. Plan the Day.** Now that you have your list and you know how much time you need to allocate for each task, you need to plot your tasks according to the time period that you want them work on them. You will need your scheduling skills for this. Do this in the morning for 5–10 minutes at the start of your day. Consider this time as your planning time so you can be more effective and more efficient throughout the day. Keep in mind though, that you have to stick to your schedule no matter what!

If an officemate stops by for a small talk, try to be polite and say that you are working on something. If that can't be helped, then give him 3–5 minutes and when that time is up, go back to your desk and start working again.

**5. Prioritize!** At the end of the day, look at your list and your schedule again. Plan for the next day and put the most important task first. When you have surmounted the biggest and most important challenge for the day, you can certainly move on with ease to the easier ones.

**6. Ask yourself: "Will it hurt for me to throw this away?"** We are inundated with emails and other forms of communication daily. No doubt, you also have lots of reports, reference materials and other documents on your desk, on your drawer, on your inbox and on your computer file folders. Most of these things add up to clutter. Clutter will make your life more difficult by slowing down your machine or by making it difficult for you to look for the more important files.

De-clutter! If you don't need a particular file or document, get rid of it. If you're a supervisor or a boss, most likely, you can still have those files when you need them.

For sure, there will be interruptions to your schedule. That can't be avoided. When there are interruptions, just deal with it and then go back to your sked. Wouldn't it be great to go back to your list at the end of the day and cross out all six items off your list?

I recommend this time management system for people who are really swamped. It is straightforward and simple. And it does not require any special tools, timer or equipment. But this is predicated and built on an important concept that Chet Holmes also put forward: what he called "pig-headed discipline and determination."

My Second System

**Get an In-basket.** This serves as the collection place for all that comes in – letters, ideas, bills, notes on a meeting, stuff I want to read – practically everything that comes my way.

**Buy lots of envelopes and folders.** Toss in some plastic organizers and boxes. By having these, you will be able to file and label all the files and references you need.

**Sweep your mind for all projects, thoughts and ideas that need action.** List down all your "open loops." You can write them on paper, then put them into the in-basket. You can process each one individually and you can identify next action steps.

**Gather all your stuff and put them in your in-basket.** Go around your room, your home office area, and even your storage spaces to gather your stuff. All of them should go into the in-basket. If an item is too big, write its name on a piece of paper and off it goes to the in-basket.

**Prepare to organize your in-basket.** Set-up your tickler file, which is essentially a calendar of 43 folders – 12 for each month of the year, and 31 envelopes for the days of the month. You will use this as a means of sending something to yourself at some time in the future.

Set up your Reference file folders/envelopes. It is better to just use one Alpha system. It might be tempting to use a lot of categories but it's simply better to file your references from A–Z. It's simple and allows you to find your files easily.

Once you've gathered all your stuff and your mental open loops, process all the items on your in basket and determine next actions. If the item does not need any action from you, you can either,

**Throw it away.** If it's trash and you will not need it anymore, then just throw it away.

**Incubate it** . Put it in the tickler file or in your Someday/Maybe lists so you can look at it again at sometime in the future.

**File it as reference.** If the item has potential value for any of your projects and for your life, it's best to file it. Get an envelope, label it properly and then put it in your reference drawer.

If an item, however, requires action from you, you can:

**Do it!** If it will take less then two minutes, do it right away!

**Delegate it.** If you're not the right person to do it, then endorse it to the right person or organization for processing.

**Defer it.** If it will take more than two minutes, you should probably put it in your calendar, depending on the priority you assign to it. If the next action step, however, is urgent or should be done anytime soon, put it in your Next Actions List for processing right away.

# SPECIFIC AREAS

### How To Manage E-mail Overload In 3 Easy Steps

Do you have control over your email, or do you suffer from email overload? You may actually be neglecting your work and losing incredible amounts of time. Many people could safely change their job to 'Email Specialist', because all they seem to do all day is send emails to and fro.

See if you recognise this story:

You're working on something and a mail comes in. You lose focus and read the email. You may be busy for five minutes writing a reply, or performing a quick task. When you're done, you have to return to the work you were doing. You need to get into your work from scratch again, losing you time again regaining your focus and flow. Getting started is the hardest part of any job and we make ourselves do it over and over by allowing email to distract us.

Tired of e-mail overload? Ready for a new way, with less time spent finishing tasks and less time handling emails – and at the same time getting more done? Let's get it on!

**Lesson One: Email is not your friend**. We instinctively look forward to email because it brings us exciting news and fun tasks. Sadly, most of the time it brings you routine stuff that just distracts you from what you could be doing. Keeping your mailbox open all the time is one of those universal habits that doesn't make any sense. If you want things to happen to you, you need to make them happen.

Email is like an unruly child that you need to take charge of. If you don't, it'll take over your life with its endless interruptions and often senseless requests. So let me show you a way to deal with email that takes only five minutes to set up. It'll help you keep your email in check and give you more space to do your real job.

**First Aid for Email Overload**

You have a serious case of email overload and you're losing the pedals. No worries, here's what to do!

Create an 'Action' folder in your inbox. Go through your mail, pick out the 10 to 15 most important ones and put them in the 'Action' folder. Work from here as long as your inbox isn't cleared. Create a 'Temporary' folder. Put your complete inbox in here. Everything! You'll be working through this in parts later, for now you can stop worrying about it. Hey presto, your inbox is empty! Add the most important email tasks to your todo list and start with Email Overload Prevention.

**Email Overload Prevention**

When dealing with email overload prevention, carry out the following steps.

Work from top to bottom, from recent to older.

Go through your COMPLETE inbox every time you open it. So don't leave your email open all the time; open it and then deal with the inbox. That means you can't just 'check your mail' anymore, there's work to be done!

Process quickly. Take one of the following actions with every mail. Don't spend more than half a minute on any given email.

Delete (as much as possible)

Archive (when it contains information you may need later) Answer (quickly, in maximum four lines) and delete/archive

Put in the 'Action' folder and add to your to do list. IMPORTANT: DO NOT work on ANY of your to dos while processing your mail! No, not even the small ones.

Clear the inbox, close your email programme or turn of the internet.

Limit your email time. Open your inbox a couple of times

a day to process it, then close it again. Only do email. Think of the Golden Rule of Productivity: choose one thing and dedicate yourself to it. There is a difference between emails and the work that they contain – keep them separated. Make a list while you process your emails, then close your email and start on the work (according to your priorities).

**Taking care of old business**

So now you've got your emails under control. Great! You're still sitting on a giant pile of emails that may or may not contain something important. Here's how you deal with it:

1. Process it in little parts. There's nothing more deadening than quickly going through hundreds of emails. Do it in little blocks of 5 minutes and it actually becomes fun! It's an ideal break from some other work, a no-brainer with instant results.

2. Use the same procedure as for your inbox. Start on top, 30 seconds max per mail, delete as much as possible, only do email...

Do this and your inbox could be cleaned within the week, and the email monster tamed. Congratulations on regaining your freedom! Here, have a badge.

**8 More Fast And Easy Techniques**

**1. Delete newsletters.** Face it: you're never going to get through all those interesting newsletters and offers. Let it go, you can find whatever you need in Google when the time is right. So delete all those daily, weekly and other digest mailers from your 'To process' and press that Unsubscribe button.

**2. Send less emails.** Call, or visit. Get your answer from the horse's mouth, and avoid endless email conversations with half the world in CC. Do not mail someone who is sitting across from you! A good test: when you feel the impulse to send a mail ask yourself: 'Can I solve this myself?' You probably can, can't you!

**3. Summarize**. Some people are addicted to email. They're like living status updates, including every thought they have and sending it to everyone even remotely connected. Very tiring, especially when they contain small to do's for you. How to deal with them? Scan the contents quickly, don't answer them and collect them in your 'Action' folder (see the previous post on email management).

Plan some time to process them. Then group them by sender, go through them in one go and write down the todos. You can even send that person an email with your list, just so they know you're on it.

**4. Send shorter emails**. Do not rewrite the bible. Long emails are tiring to read and no one really gets what you're saying anyway. Less is more. **Keep it under 4 sentences.** Or how about this for a short answer: resist the urge to answer at all. If you want a friendly chat with lots of fluff, call them.

**5. Check your emails less**. 3 to 5 times a day should do it. You can always be on top of things and make sure everything is take care of. Even better: you can let things run their course while you get your work done.

**6. Make rules**. You could apply a CC filter that makes mails that aren't addressed directly to you go to a separate folder. You can plan some time to go through it, without wasting time on email conversations. Stop being irritated with it, just ignore it.

**7. Feel free to delete a lot of emails** . Emails are like stuff in the attic: very hard to get rid of. What if you ever need any of it again? I can personally say that I've hardly ever needed any of my emails again, and when I did I found another way to deal with the situation. Live in the present, let go of the past. You can do it!

**8. Avoid working double**. When you get the same question all the time, write down your answer in a document or email template. Or put it on the website, and refer to it in your answer.

**Telecommuting: How To Increase Productivity From Home**

Congratulations, you can work from home! It's a great freedom to be able to combine your household with work, to not have to commute... But with freedom comes responsibility. What if you spend all day caught up in home affairs? Or you're sitting there in your pyjamas with no-one to check on you and you find you're not getting much done at all?

**1. Create a divide between home and work**. It can make a world of difference to have a separate work space. Ideally, you have an office or studio at home or in the neighbourhood. Failing that, just a room with a door you can close.

**2. Put on your work clothes**. Don't keep running around in your pajamas! Dress like you would at work. Because you know what? You actually are. The clothes bring you in the right mood to work, and it's a lot less embarrassing when your colleague pays you an unexpected visit.

**3. Be extremely punctual**. So you don't need to do traffic jams – enjoy that extra cup of coffee! At the same time, respect the working hours that you've set out for yourself. If not, you could end up being one of those people that loafs around all day and then when there's fun to be had, 'has to finish something'. Shame!

**4. Don't watch TV**. Don't go to the movies, or the launderette. You're working, so work. Of course, be sure to take a well-deserved break now and again and remind yourself how great it is to work from home.

**5. Go out to lunch**. Working from home is liberating but

also isolating. Keep in touch with your friends and colleagues, forge new connections and connect to the world by going out to lunch. Better yet, go to business networking lunches!

**6. Have someone to answer to.** It's easier to work when there's someone watching and when we need to justify our time. So get one of these mechanisms to work for you (without making it disagreeable). Ask on of your colleagues or friends to check on you.

### Meetings

Here are our short and sweet suggestions for meetings:

-- Hold as little of them as possible. -- Make them as short as possible.

-- Don't do 'e-mail meetings', i.e., CC'ing everybody and making it a group discussion. -- Have an agenda.

-- Have someone take short notes and especially, write down practical todo's. -- Learn to speak concisely.

-- Think solutions, not problems.

-- Stick to the subject, don't bring up other stuff.

Here is some more material

Meetings... Lots of them are short and sweet. But a whole lot more are long, tedious and boring! Might you have attended a boring meeting once in your life? And wondered: what's the use?!

**A meeting is a gathering of two or more people to achieve a common purpose or goal.** At the end of a meeting, you and your organization should have come up with a better understanding of a problem or a situation, or a set of actions that must be taken.

Here are some **guidelines** to keep in mind when facilitating and managing a meeting.

### Before the meeting

Know the purpose of the meeting. Why are you calling for a meeting? Take a minute to think about the outcome you would like:

-- To inform the members or officers of the organization about anything that affects the organization.

-- To discuss ways to achieve goals and objectives. -- To plan for an upcoming event.

-- To get clarification and monitor progress of ongoing projects. -- To resolve problems and settle disputes.

-- To make decisions.

Once you know the purpose of the meeting, you need to write down the **agenda**. It will help you focus on the tasks that must be accomplished in the meeting and prevent you from being sidetracked by other matters.

Identify the **participants** to the meeting. Will this be a meeting for the officers only? Do you need to involve all members of the organization? Is it a General Assembly? An emergency meeting for decision-makers? Do you need to invite other people to serve as resource persons? As you go through the agenda, you will be able to identify who exactly needs to go to the meeting.

If you know the participants to the meeting, you will also be able to anticipate how they will react to the issues to be raised in the meeting. This is called '**Lining up the ducks**': prepare your arguments and case in such a way that it will meet the minimum of resistance.

Set the **time and venue,** and then **send out the invitation** for the meeting to the people concerned. The venue should be conducive to the kind of meeting you will be organizing. For creative endeavors, you could do outdoor meetings – perhaps in a park or any place that stimulates creativity. It could also be the office of one of your colleagues. This should include the items on the agenda so that they could prepare for discussion and materials they may need to bring to the meeting.

**Prepare all the handouts, materials and equipment you need**. Reports need to be printed and photocopied and/or encoded in a Powerpoint presentation. Projectors, microphones, writing pads, pens and recording devices should be present in the meeting room before the meeting starts.

**Rules of Order**

When you are meeting ten people or less, it is easy to give everyone a chance to speak, listen to arguments presented and decide on important matters. But if you are meeting twenty, fifty or a hundred people, it becomes difficult. You will need a Rules of Order. If your organization has one, then use it. If not, it could be handy to make one for future meetings.

**During the meeting**

**Start on time.** Set a new standard of professionalism. When you start on time, even if not everyone is there yet, you are showing people that you respect people's time. And you also show that you intend not to wait for those who don't respect your time.

Go through each item of the agenda. Avoid distractions as much as possible.

**Facilitate discussions smoothly**. This means giving everyone a chance to speak. Don't let anyone dominate the discussion and the meeting. Otherwise, other people will not be able to air their thoughts and opinions.

**Sidestep endless discussion.** Don't let people take over the meeting, or go on a tangent. Some discussions can't be won. Defer to another time, keep your purpose for the meeting firmly in mind.

**Record the discussions.** Thank you mp3 players and laptop computers! Don't forget to transcribe it soon though. If you don't put in writing, you will soon forget about it.

**Take the Minutes of the Meeting.** Taking minutes of the meeting could be as simple as jotting down highlights of discussions and the actions taken. Or it could be a formal Minutes of the Proceedings. Formal minutes and proceedings can include the following items:

-- Title of the meeting, including the date and time. -- List of all members present during the meeting.

-- List of members who sent their apologies for their absence.

-- Confirmation that the minutes of the previous meeting had been accepted and agreed as accurate record.

-- Amendments to the minutes of the previous meeting.

-- Matters that arose from the minutes of the previous meeting should be listed down in the order that they were discussed in the meeting.

-- The actions taken for each of the items in the agenda. In some instances, the number of votes for decisions must be noted down, too.

-- The time of the adjournment.

**After the meeting**

**Summarize the decisions made and next steps that must be taken.** You can just look at the minutes of the meeting and you will easily see the next steps that must be taken. List down these action steps and identify the right person who can do it. If you don't do this right away, the members of the organization may forget about it.

**Send out the minutes to the members.** When you do this, you can include the list of action steps and the people in charge of them. Remind the members of their commitment to these action items.

If you catch yourself in too many meetings, you probably need to review your minutes. Look at the action steps if they are being done. If not, then that means that you should probably be implementing the results of the meetings, instead of holding another meeting.

# PART 5: MAKING TECHNOLOGY WORK FOR YOU

# THE USE OF TECHNOLOGY

This chapter is not about how to use your latest iPad or smart watch; nor will it tell you which devices you should buy or use in various situations. Rather, it warns you that technology steals time as well as saves time, and suggests how you can use it to your advantage without allowing it to vacuum time from other meaningful activities. Computer games, social media, the Internet, and even e-mail, if not controlled, will not only consume unrealistic amounts of time, but can become addictive, and in excess, can negatively impact your health and well-being. We have a limited amount of time at our disposal, and using excessive amounts of it on these digital innovations can leave inadequate time for such necessities as sleep, exercise and relationships. This in turn can result in excessive stress, reduced performance, and health issues that offset many of the productivity gains made by technology.

This book reviews the good, the bad and the ugly of technology, identifies how and where it consumes excessive amounts of time, and suggests how we can manage the use of technology so we can take advantage of all its benefits without suffering any ill effects. This will involve making wise choices, practicing self-discipline and doing what doesn't seem to come naturally – taking control of your life. This is possible since you're in possession of a priceless piece of technology, which will never be surpassed by any future innovation created by man – your brain. Control your brain and you control yourself. Control yourself, and you control technology. Control technology, and you have your life back.

**The good of technology**

There is little problem outlining the "good" of technology. Most of us have experienced the ease with which we can obtain information, directions and advice, perform calculations, solve problems, and even contact people around the world in a matter of seconds at little or no cost. We don't have to write – or even type – in order to communicate. We no longer have to search for telephone numbers, memorize – or in many cases, even think. It is all done *for* us. The "good" of technology is evident almost everywhere – at home, at school, at work or while travelling. It benefits students, teachers, business managers & entrepreneurs, and people from all walks of life, whether young or old. Although seniors may not be as fully immersed in technology as others, they certainly benefit from it. They have access to medication – dispensing systems that not only remind them when to take their pills, but in some cases even inform the doctor if they don't. Smart watches can track their daily activities, and even detect heart attacks – sending alerts if something's not right. Sensor carpets can help identify when a person has fallen. All of these technological innovations help to keep seniors out of hospitals and seniors homes, enabling them to remain at home and self-manage their chronic conditions. The *Ontario Telemedicine Network* (ontariotelehomecare.otn.ca) provides technology which allows patients to measure their vital signs at home – things such as weight, blood pressure and blood oxygen – with the results being monitored by specially-trained nurses or respiratory therapists. Long-distance medicine, or telemedicine as it is normally called, is also made possible through technology. It is a relatively new field in which the doctor and patient may never meet or even interact in real time. One example is *Grand Rounds*, an elite network of physicians in the U.S. who deliver second opinions on treatment plans and diagnoses for baffling ailments. No doubt the virtual medicine will expand as it bridges the gap between patient demand and physician availability – especially since it can access doctors with specialized experience and track records.

And look what technology has done for the physically handicapped. The Internet allows sick and physically handicapped people who may be isolated by their lack of complete mobility to connect online. Scientists can insert a chip into the brain of a patient who is totally paralyzed and connect it to a computer, so that through thought alone, that patient can surf the web, read and write e-mails, play videogames, control their wheelchair, operate household appliances and manipulate mechanical arms. It boggles the mind to think that it is now possible for the brain to interface with a computer and control any object around it.

Computers will even handle your investments. "Robo advisors" are automated investing services that rely on computer models to manage portfolios. Older folks can really appreciate the marvels of technology while younger people take it for granted. Imagine being able to deposit checks into ATM machines with no paperwork or even an envelope, and withdraw money with a touch of a few buttons. We no longer have to type; but simply dictate to our laptops using voice activated software. We store our files in the cloud, ask Siri for directions or glance at our GPS. We can shop for groceries, clothing, and electronics – literally anything – without leaving our chair. We can choose any movie, sporting event or educational program we want and do it through our TV set or portable device. We can keep ourselves entertained online with jigsaw puzzles, crosswords, games or Sudoku. We can't brew coffee on our laptops yet, but we can listen to the background noises of a coffee shop at coffitivity.com while we sip our automatically brewed coffee.

But it all comes at a cost.

**The bad of technology**

The younger generation cannot see anything bad about technology because they have nothing to compare it to. Nor can they fully appreciate the benefits, because they have never experienced anything else. They were born into it. There is little doubt that technology is rewiring our brains. Because of the plasticity of our brains, *any* experience will rewire them to some degree; but we spend so much time with digital technology that it is having a much greater impact. There are many cases of physical changes to the brain caused by repetitively performing one type of task for long periods of time, which could be either good or bad depending on the results. And as far as I know, there's nothing bad about that. For example, taxi drivers were found to have a larger hippocampus, an area of the brain associated with context, navigational skills and spatial memory. This was caused by their continuous task of navigating the complex network of streets in the city. Similarly, the brains of virtuoso violinists, athletes, and other performers show a measurable increase in size of those areas associated with the particular skill that they are continually practising. It makes sense that continually playing video games will also strengthen those skills needed to excel in the particular games being played. What those areas are, and whether any such skills are transferrable are not yet clear. Although at least one neuroscientist has suggested that the person would do well if he or she were hired to play video games. Unfortunately, video games have been found to increase blood pressure and heart rate and activate the stress response. Research also indicates that extensive video gaming makes youngsters more aggressive and desensitizes them to violence. There also have been at least two documented cases of death occurring while playing video games – both cardiac arrests – and one of them being a 19 year-old – but who knows if there weren't pre-existing conditions.

A survey of gamers aged 10 to 19 that revealed that they spent 30% less time reading and 34% less time doing homework.

There are a few things becoming evident with the increase in screen use and digital technology in general. We are becoming more easily distracted, ADHD symptoms appear to be increasing, some of us are becoming addicted to computer games, email and/or the Internet, and evidence seems to suggest we are becoming less empathetic, more shallow in our thinking, and more open to health problems such as obesity and heart disease. And of course some people are experiencing cyber bullying, occasionally leading to anxiety or suicide, and there is evidence of a few cases of death by gaming; but these are rare occurrences.

Nicholas Carr, in his book, *Shallows: what the Internet is doing to our brains*, claims he has noticed changes in his own reading. He loses concentration after a page or two, becomes fidgety, loses track of the storyline and looks for something else to do.

In the past decade, Internet use has expanded by 566%. It is estimated that 40% of all people of the world are now online. By 2012 we were searching for information via Google more than 1 trillion times each year. We "liked" 4.5 billion items on Facebook and uploaded hundreds of hours of video on YouTube for every minute of real time. With over 6 billion cell phones in use, and the average teenager, according to Nielsen research, sending about 4000 text messages each month, it is not difficult to imagine the impact on our brain. B oundaries are no longer defined by technology, but by our own biology. A survey of workplaces showed workers were being interrupted every three minutes, and people have an average of eight windows open at the same time.

Ed Hallowell, who has written several books related to ADD and ADHD, coined the expression "attention deficit trait" to describe the ADHD – like symptoms being displayed by adults and induced by a business environment that is now characterized by a fast pace, rapid change, constant interruptions and information overload. Absorbing new information also burns energy. And it takes even more energy to multi-task, make decisions and work on demanding tasks. To maximize brain efficiency, we must protect our brain from energy- draining activities encouraged, if not caused, by technology. Getting more things done faster is no longer limited by the lack of technology, but by our brain. Our brain has a limited capacity for processing information, and this limit is being approached and frequently passed by the ever-increasing rate at which it is being assaulted by new information. Just as watering a potted plant too fast with too much water causes much of the water to overflow, so too much information coming at us too quickly from every direction causes much of it to be lost. We miss receiving it, can't store it or quickly forget it. And the information we lose could be important or even critical. The more we rely on computers to control critical systems such as airline routes, electricity grids, financial markets, street traffic lights, lines of communication and other aspects of our lives, the greater the more helpless we are when computers crash. One example is the incident on July 8, 2015, when as chance would have it, American Airlines were forced to ground all their flights, the New York Stock Exchange halted all trading, and the Wall Street Journal also experienced computer problems – all on the same day. In my 43 years I have forgotten to pick up bread on the way home from work and struggled to recall a name several times, but have yet to experience brain outages of those proportions.

**The ugly of technology**

The really ugly, is beyond comprehension, and hopefully will never occur. I am referring here to scenarios where we could become a race of non-thinking humans, easily controlled by others .Artificial intelligence will eventually exceed our own, or at least when we die in the flesh, our minds will be uploaded to a computer and remain conscious. Nobody knows for sure the ultimate impact of the new technology. But we do know it seems to have a life of its own, regardless of the degree of good, bad and ugly, and we are unable to stop or slow down the ever- increasing speed of change even if we wanted to do so. The time it takes for a new technology to be adopted by 50 million people, referred to as the rate of penetration, is decreasing rapidly. For example, it took 38 years for radio, 20 years for the telephone, 13 years for TV, and only four years for the World Wide Web. Facebook took 3.6 years, the iPad, two years, and Google Plus only 88 days. *The future of the mind* , that it took 350 years since the invention of the telescope to enter the space age, but it has taken only 15 years since the introduction of the MRI and advanced brain scans to actively connect the brain to the outside world. Now, many of us are quick to adopt a new technology, regardless of its merit, for fear of being left behind. And we are becoming so reliant on digital technology that we are spending more time in the virtual world than the real world. O nline sales are projected to account for 10% of all retail sales in the United States. 58% of all Americans play videogames. U.S. Internet users spend 22.5% of their online time on social networking sites or blogs. More than a third of the couples who married between 2005 and 2012 in the U.S. reported meeting their spouse online.

What's ugly about that? Well, only that the trend towards the virtual world will continue, and that we are passing these habits onto the next generation who may never know what they're missing by not actively playing outdoors, having fun in the rain, enjoying the company of others in real time, communing with nature and growing in mind, body and spirit as they create their own games and learn to cope with problems on their own. Of course, they won't know any different so perhaps the ugliness is only in my own mind. But I think the Internet is a place you go to in order to find information; after which you leave – like we used to do with hardcopy encyclopaedias. In short, using technology without being absorbed by it.

**Using technology**

The purpose of this chapter is not to debate the advantages and disadvantages of technology, because the rapid progression of technology, good, bad or ugly is a fact of life. What I want to do is offer some suggestions as to how to take advantage of what technology has to offer, while avoiding any accompanying time traps and health and lifestyle issues that many people are experiencing. We are fortunate inasmuch as we are a part of the only generation, assuming you're over 25, who know what it was like *before* the current digital age of speed. We can judge for ourselves what is helpful and what is not, and we can actually reject certain high-tech devices or methods if we feel they are not for us. Future generations will not have that luxury. When I was born, radio was already a fact of life. I didn't question it; because that's just the way it was. But I never saw a TV set until I was in my early teens, and the first cell phone did not appear until 1980s. Now there are 6.8 billion cell phone subscribers worldwide. My mother used to tell us to get our ears away from the radio and to go play outside in the fresh air. Science and modern medicine have long ago proven the wisdom of that suggestion. Parenting hasn't changed that much – except many younger parents already use iPads as babysitters. Sitting in the airport a few weeks ago I took a picture – with my iPad of course – of a young father and his toddler sitting side-by-side, each engrossed in their respective handheld devices. This is not a statement about the merit of iPads, it is a question about the *use* of iPads. How you use technology determines the impact of technology on your life. And how you use it is determined by your mindset. There is a scripture reference that urges us, "Do not conform any longer to the pattern of this world, but be transformed by the renewing of your mind." The key is to continue renewing your mind, not to outsource it to technology. Any invention, from the Guttenberg press, the automobile and the first typewriter to modern day computers, has consumed some of our time, especially through the initial stages of the learning curve. The difference in digital technology is that it consumes such huge amounts of our time. Everyone seems to have a shortage of time these days. Every adult and child seems to own multiple devices that they use for entertainment, information, socializing and communication.

# RUNNING OUT OF TIME?

### The Internet, social media, and TV

Television, the number one leisure activity in the world, consumes over half of our free time and is accused of stealing time away from our friendships and relationships with people. The Internet has joined the TV set in vacuuming up more of our time. In 1998, studies concluded that the more that people used the Internet, the less they communicated with their families and friends, and the greater the increase of loneliness and depression. Several years later, with the introduction of social networking sites, this changed somewhat inasmuch as we started communicating and socializing more; but with little if any personal face-to-face contact. *Facebook* , the largest social networking site, was launched at *Harvard University* in 2004. By 2009, there were over 250 million people in 170 countries and territories on every continent, and almost half its users visited the site every day. A *Toronto Globe & Mail* article, July 22, 2010, announced that membership had hit 500 million that year and that its members were spending roughly 700 billion minutes there. At that time they were adding 50 million users each month and getting 100 billion hits per day.

In 2014, Facebook boasted 1.32 billion active users spending an average of 40 minutes a day on this one social media giant.

Although 40 minutes a day seems like a long time, it is nothing compared to the 5 hours a day consumed by television. And at least there is more social interaction while communicating on Facebook than there is in being glued to a TV set. Two million friends are requested every twenty minutes and three million messages are sent during that same time period. Social networking is now the fourth most popular online activity, ahead of email and behind search engines, general Internet portals such as Yahoo & AOL, and software downloads. The amount of time spent using social networking sites is growing three times the rate of overall Internet usage.

**Email**

Another thing that consumes our time is email. A Canadian Health report (mentioned in the book, *Sleep to be Sexy, Smart & Slim* by Ellen Michaud with Julie Bain) claims that more than a half of all employees take work home, 69% check their email from home, 59% check voice mail after hours and 29% keep their cell phones on day and night. As a result, 46% feel that this work-related intrusion is a stressor and 44% report negative spill over onto their families. (And the families are supposed to be the most effective buffer to workplace stress.) Work is no longer a place, but a state of mind. Our work goes with us wherever we go – if not in our hand, then in a computer bag or holstered on our hip. With smartphones and tablets, it's easier to be a workaholic these days. According to Dr. Julian Ford and Jon Wortman, author of *Hijacked by your brain* , 37.8% of professional men and 14.4% of women are already working more than 50 hours per week. The average working professional spends roughly 23% of the workday on email, and glances at the inbox about 36 times an hour according to the book, *The Power of Forgetting* by Mike Byster (2014).

Email can be addictive – like continually pulling the handle on a slot machine to bring a person that much closer to a payoff. Psychologists call it "operant conditioning" – a term used to describe any voluntary behavior that is shaped by its consequences. The consequence of repetitively checking email is receiving the occasional email that is of interest. The use of texting, which is even faster and more intrusive than email, is on the increase, particularly among the younger generation. According to research by Nielson, and reported in the book, *The end of absence: reclaiming what we've lost in a world of constant connection* , by Michael Harris, the average teenager now manages upward of 4000 text messages every month. If we were to be more attentive to whatever project we were working on at the time, had a greater power of focus, and were not so easily distracted. The same thing applies to smartphone and Internet use and other work habits.

**Video and computer games**

Unlike email, computer games are designed to be addictive, like the slot machines in Las Vegas, and researchers in 2005 found that dopamine levels in players' brains doubled while they were playing. Dopamine is the hormone associated with mood and feelings of pleasure. A 2012 study of adolescents, reported that boys between the ages of 10 to 13 were playing video games an average of 43 hours a week. Video gaming has also become a popular spectator sport – evidently more popular than the World Series, with 32 million people watching the League of Legends World Championship while only about 15 million tuned into the World Series last year. The audience for gaming is expected to increase to 170 million by 2017. Evidently you become a better gamer if you watch the experts. And there is a gradual increase in the number of adults spending significant amounts of time on video games as well. If we are spending so much time watching TV, surfing the Internet, watching YouTube videos, playing electronic games, checking email, talking or texting on smartphones and participating in social media, where do people get the time to do all this?

# DEPLETED BY TECHNOLOGY

**Where is the time coming from?**
Thankfully, a lot of time is generated by technology itself as it speeds up mundane but essential tasks, streamlines communications, eliminates the necessity of doing many routine activities and automates everything from opening tin cans to garage doors. Unfortunately, using technology in many cases has become an end in itself, with about half the time being spent on digital media being stolen from health-related and lifestyle activities such as exercise, sleep, family time, leisure time and one-on-one relationships. These in turn negatively impact our personal productivity as well as our health and lifestyle.

**Real time relationships**
A survey conducted in 1985 where people were asked "Over the last six months, who are the people with whom you discussed matters important to you?" The most common number of friends listed was three. When the same survey was used in 2004 the most common number of such friends listed was zero. Smartphones are definitely interfering with relationships. When one person in the relationship is frequently checking email or text messages it is sending a signal that what he or she is doing on their cell phone is more important than interacting with the other person. One study from *Brigham Young University* found that of 143 women in relationships, the majority reported that cell phones, computers, and other devices were significantly interrupting their relationships and family lives.

**Sleep**
Sleep is one of the first things to suffer if a person needs more time to get things done. In my lifetime, the average amount of sleep we get has decreased from just over eight

hours to 6.7 hours. (More recently I read a figure of 6.5 hours, along with an explanation that this is the average amount of sleep people *say* they get but by the measurement of brain activity while these same people were sleeping, the *actual* figure was 6.1 hours.) If you get less than six hours sleep a night you are considered to be sleep deprived. After six hours of sleep or less you could experience sleepiness, a tired feeling, trouble concentrating, headaches and even nausea. Warning signs could also include changes in your mood such as apathy, fatigue, anxiety, nervousness, irritability and depression. You could be more forgetful than usual, make more mistakes, drive more erratically and anger more easily. Most doctors seem to recommend between seven hours and nine hours a night and not less than six. Seven seems to be the ideal number that crops up in research again and again, although everyone isn't the same. According to the West Virginia research team, sleeping less than five hours a night, including naps, more than doubles the risk of being diagnosed with angina, coronary heart disease, heart attack or stroke. Calcified arteries were found in 27% of those who slept less than five hours a night. S leep deprivation is one of the risk factors in Alzheimer's. S leep helps clear the brain, flushing away waste products such as Alzheimer's-related proteins. One sleep scientist claims that sleep is one of the most important predictors of how long you will live – as important as whether you smoke, exercise or have high blood pressure. Depriving yourself of sufficient sleep also affects your energy level. Sleep is the only time when your brain can produce ATP, a substance that stores and delivers energy in cells.

And if you're wondering by now what health and wellness have to do with personal productivity, from a time management perspective, both illness and death are a complete waste of time.

**Exercise**

Exercise is another activity that is easily sacrificed as people feel pressured by a lack of time. The best thing for strengthening working memory and long-term memory, as well as other cognitive skills, is to continually exercise both your body and your brain. You need to keep the blood flowing to the brain with the oxygen and glucose that it needs in order to operate at its peak. The brain may be only 2% of the weight of the body, but it consumes up to 25% of the overall glucose and blood circulation. According to Statistics Canada, only 13% of Canadian adults aged 49 to 59 and 11% of those aged 60 and above meet the guidelines for moderate physical activity (defined as 150 minutes of moderate to vigorous activity per week in bouts of 10 minutes or more, in addition to muscle and bone strengthening activities using major muscle groups at least two days a week). The benefits of physical activity was highlighted when researchers in Australia published results of trials conducted with 170 older adults who had started showing memory problems and had increased risk of developing dementia. The participants averaged an extra 29 minutes a day of physical activity over six months. The experimental group scored better on tests of their cognition than the control group and was twice as great as the one that had previously been shown with the drug Aricept, which is currently being used to slow the progression of Alzheimer's disease. And the improvement lasted for 12 months after the exercise program ended. The explanation is that exercising the heart somehow stimulates growth factors to produce more new nerve cells in the hippocampus, one of the key centers in the brain for memory and learning. It stands to reason that the more time you spend at computers or in front of TV sets, the less exercise you are getting, and this is evident in the increase in obesity in North America.

**Multitasking**

Yes, multitasking can free up time under certain circumstances, as I will explain later. But the price you pay is the risk of reduced attention and quality and the resulting impact could wipe out or exceed any gains. In their haste to get things done, more and more people are attempting to multitask inappropriately. Technology encourages and provides more opportunities to multitask. A smartphone, for example, might allow you to leave work early and watch your son's soccer game; but you are still connected to your office and not fully present while your son is performing on the field.

# HOW TO MANAGE TECHNOLOGY

**Make good choices**

Technology was not *meant* to infringe on relationships, family time, sleep or exercise. Nor was it expected to weaken executive skills such as attention and emotional control. Technology was meant to increase our personal productivity, make us more efficient and free up discretionary time so we are not slaves to our work. But in many cases we have become slaves to technology. Technology was meant to be a means to an end but in many cases it is being used as an end in itself. It has opened up new ways to spend our time such as online gaming, gambling and surfing the Internet. The convenience of digital technology has its costs. And if not managed, the cost in terms of personal health as well as personal productivity could be high. We could make suggestions for managing email and electronic files and review keyboard shortcuts, and so on; but they would be of little value if you are unable or unwilling to resist the temptation to buy into every new device or update that hits the market or limit your use of the non-productive games, social media, videos and websites that bombard all of us on a daily basis. The fact is, we can't do everything. Time management in the digital age of speed involves making wise choices. And it's difficult to make wise choices when we do our thinking with sleep-deprived brains – sleep-deprived because we don't have enough time after our over-involvement with digital technology to sleep properly, exercise sufficiently or eat nutritionally. An online poll of over 1000 Canadian adults released by *Angus Reid/Vision Critical* ( *Toronto Star* , January 26, 2013) revealed that 90% of the respondents believed their smartphones made their lives more convenient. So convenient, evidently, that 30% of them go online before getting out of bed, 31% use them at the dinner table, 29% actually use them in the washroom and 42% use them just before falling asleep at night. In this chapter and in those following, I will suggest some strategies that you might take to prevent digital technology from becoming all-consuming. This does not mean you should ignore technology; it means you should use it responsibly so that you don't ignore your life.

**Protect your relationships**

I already mentioned the impact that smartphone use is having on relationships, and that they are already a topic of discussion in some marriage counselling sessions. Being shunned, ignored or rejected is painful, and functional MRIs actually reveal that both physical pain and rebuff or rejection share the same pathways in the brain. It is even believed that these seemingly minor hurts through inattention or rejection are cumulative. Over time, they can fester to the point of compromising physical and mental health. First you must decide what is important in your life and developing personal policies or guidelines to protect those activities. One thing that is being affected by technology is time for personal one-on-one relationships. If both parties in a relationship are guilty of using their smart phones while together – such as in restaurants, at family gatherings or in the bedroom – communications will suffer, and communications is usually considered essential to a happy relationship. Action has to be taken to protect those times together. Such action could include setting some boundaries and guidelines that are acceptable to both parties. We all need time for technology – both for business and personal reasons – but it should not overlap with time being spent together. Perhaps there could be specific times when both partners work independently for an hour or so. There could be a policy of no cell phones during specific activities such as mealtimes, during dates, and at bedtime. You could decide to turn off cell phones and laptops at a specific time in the evening or have technology-free hours during the day. And never set a place for technology at the dinner table. The important thing is to assess the impact, if any, that cell phones and other devices are having on your relationships, health and use of time, and take any necessary action. The impact on others should be considered; but the final decisions are yours to make.

**Manage your email**

If email is consuming too much time, you could set up a time and a procedure for handling email. Don't allow it to control your day. You might check email twice per day, for instance – more frequently if your company's success depends on a quick response to emails. Checking your email every five minutes or so is both costly and time consuming. It's not generally a good idea to check email first thing in the morning. You could easily get distracted from your plan. But if you make it part of your plan to check email first just to ensure there are no vital and urgent items there, that's not such a bad idea. You may decide not to respond to email until about 11 or 11:30 a.m. You could check it again about 3:30 in the afternoon. You might want to turn off the automatic send/receive option so that email doesn't pop up in your inbox the moment you sign on. Email programs seem to be designed to control *us* rather than the other way around. I encourage everyone to at least give it a try. Check your email twice per day for at least a couple of days and then assess the impact on your business. I'm sure most people have experienced a computer crash or an Internet access problem or a vacation when accessing email was impossible, and yet we survived the experience with no earth-shattering problems.

**Don't stay glued to your chair**

Your health is important; certainly more important than time management. When you are sick, you couldn't care less about managing your time or personal productivity or technology. You just want to get better. All your time is devoted to getting well, and personal productivity as it relates to business comes to a standstill. So it stands to reason that health is the most important time management strategy. We have already mentioned how digital technology is interfering with sleep, exercise and nutrition and a few of the possible consequences such as obesity, high blood pressure, stress, ADHD symptoms and other health issues. And that it is imperative that you cut out marathon work sessions, working through lunch, using digital technology well into the evening and failing to take regular breaks. But there also is an indication of physical problems emerging as a result of overuse of digital technology as well. The first of these to become evident was carpal tunnel syndrome and we have already made adjustments with the way we use our mouse, position the hand, and support our wrist. But research published by Kenneth Hansraj in the *National Library of Medicine,* and reported in the *Toronto Star* , November 24, 2014, indicates that bending your neck over a smart phone for hours a day could lead to early wear and tear on the spine, degeneration and even surgery. And smartphone users spend an average of 2 to 4 hours a day hunched over, reading e-mails, sending texts or checking the social media sites. Known as *text neck* , this problem is caused by an increase in the weight of the head as it bends forward. The weight on the cervical spine varies from 27 pounds at a 15° angle to 60 pounds at a 60° angle. So posture, height of chair and amount of time sitting in front of your computer are all factors that should be considered. If you're sitting at your computer all day you can't be getting much exercise. A February, 2013 Australian survey of over 63,000 middle-aged men found that those who sat for more than four hours a day, were significantly more likely to have chronic diseases like high blood pressure and heart disease. You might consider getting a stand-up desk as well. Tom Rath, in his book *Eat Move Sleep*, (Missionday, 2013) called sitting "the most underrated health threat of modern times." He claims that *sitting* more than six hours a day greatly increases your risk of an early death. An article in the November, 2014 *Scientific American* proves this is not just a case of shock journalism. The author of the article, James Levine, co-directs *Obesity Solutions*, a program of the *Mayo Clinic* in Scottsdale Arizona. The title of his article is "Killer chairs," and he gives some statistics based on 18 studies reported during the past 16 years, covering 800,000 people – in addition to his own research. He had a few eye-opening findings showing that sitting for over 4 hours a day contributes to diabetes, obesity, and cardiovascular problems Neither Tom Rath nor James Levine seem to be suggesting jogging or marathon walks to remedy the problem, but rather to just get out of your chair. Get up and move around, as we were created to do, rather than lead a sedentary life. Walk around while you talk on the phone, work at a stand-up desk, have stand-up meetings, take the stairs instead of the elevator, walk to the local mall instead of taking the car – are the type of recommendations these authors seem to be supporting.

Don't overlook the health issues, and above all, take frequent stretch breaks.

# MULTITASKING

**Multitask with caution**

By multitasking, I mean the *apparent* simultaneous performance of two or more tasks. And since research has confirmed that it is impossible for the brain to *fully* focus on two things at the same time, there is really no such thing as multitasking. People who think they are doing two jobs simultaneously, such as listening on the telephone while signing documents are deceiving themselves. The brain cannot do two tasks at the same time. It actually switches rapidly back and forth between one task and the other. Although the brain is only absent from either task for a fraction of a second, that brief absence could result in serious consequences. Dr. Amir AllenTowfigh, a neurologist with *Weill Cornell Medical Center* claims that attempts at multitasking can jam up your brain processing. He says our frontal lobes are the main engines directing our attention, and they have a limited amount of processing power. Multitasking puts a strain on working memory since it requires you to bring back important pieces of information for each task as you switch back and forth between them. By using functional MRI, researchers discovered that when people juggle two assignments, their prefrontal cortex appeared to deal with the tasks one at a time, creating this mental bottleneck. Brain research does indicate that you can have several motor programs running simultaneously, whether it's steering your car, talking on your cell phone, texting a message or whatever; but you can only focus your conscious attention fully on one thing at a time. Your body may react through habit; but your brain thinks sequentially. So relying on muscle memory when thinking is required can be a dangerous practice. Multitasking can also be stressful, and during stress our weakest executive skills become more pronounced. Too much exertion without a break taxes the executive skills as well. In most cases the cards are stacked against you when you multitask. But there are situations where you can multitask (or perform rapid brain switching) and increase your performance without the fear of serious negative consequences; because all multitasking is not the same.

**All multitasking is not the same**

There are three types or degrees of multitasking. Let's look at the three types or degrees of multitasking in increasing order of efficiency. The first and most obviously inefficient, and potentially dangerous, form of multitasking involves physically performing two tasks at the same time – both requiring cognitive involvement – such as talking on a cell phone while driving through city traffic, or text messaging while listening to a lecture on safety procedures. The second type involves working on a routine task *physically* , while *thinking* about something else, such as planning your day while taking a shower or mentally rehearsing a speech as you collate reports or worrying about finances as you put away the dishes. Frequently the motor part of the multitasking becomes almost automatic through repetition. The third type involves what we used to refer to as a "utilizing idle time" – checking e-mail while a report is being printed or making a phone call while clothes are being dried or listening to information on your iPod while getting your hair done in a salon. Only the first two are true multitasking, while the third one is simply making efficient use of time that might otherwise be wasted. This is not really multitasking and the worst that might happen is to forget to retrieve the printed page from the printer or forget to remove your clothes from the dryer. The seriousness of the second type of multitasking depends on the tasks involved. Daydreaming, while operating a machine or crossing the street in traffic is dangerous; but listening to the radio while taking a shower is not usually a problem. After all what's the big deal if you miss the temperature report or forget to shampoo your hair? But the fact is, you do get more accomplished in terms of quantity when you multitask. But the quality is not there. And there could be time-consuming – or even disastrous results.

The good news is that by the time I finish this chapter you will have completed your email, and if you add the 85% performance on one task to the 45% on the other task, you would have actually performed at 130% by your attempt at doing two tasks simultaneously. You have to be the judge as to whether any multitasking is beneficial or harmful, and that's why I emphasized that there are different degrees of multitasking. Missing or misunderstanding what I say, or failing to provide a complete answer to an e-mailer's question might not be important. But I don't suggest you mentally rehearse a speech while strapping a child into a car seat. The impact of irresponsible multitasking is now so obvious that it cannot be ignored. The *Human Factors and Ergonomics Society* estimates that 2600 deaths and 330,000 injuries are caused each year by motorists speaking on their cell phones while driving. M ultitasking also disrupts the kind of sustained thought usually required for problem-solving and creativity. So if you decide to conserve time by working on two tasks at the same time, be sure to consider the impact of making a mistake or missing something. On the other hand, don't be paranoid and sit idly by while a 50-page document is being printed.

# TIME STRATEGY

**Schedule your priorities**

The practice of scheduling is becoming more important than ever. Thanks to technology, we are so overloaded with options for using our limited time that it has now become necessary to schedule everything from time at the gym to time for spontaneity. Scheduling is a great way of protecting the time for activities that are important and meaningful to you. You know you can't do everything; but you can do anything. That's where wise choices come into play. Once you have identified certain projects or activities as being important to you, such as writing a book, learning a new language, developing a new product, exercise, family activities and so on, you can schedule time for those activities in your planner – early in the day or week if feasible. If you run out of time, it is the lesser important activities that lose by default, not the important or critical ones such as those that relate to a healthy body, mind and spirit, including relationships. How tragic would it really be if you didn't tweet this week or failed to check Facebook or didn't watch a YouTube video?

**Use a planner for your scheduling**

You can do your planning and scheduling on a high-tech digital device, but scheduling is so important that I choose not to do so. Using a paper planner serves to ground me in reality. I can touch it and feel it and see my scheduled projects the moment I open it. Writing down an appointment solidifies that meeting in my mind; dictating it to a handheld device makes little impact, little commitment, and little chance I will even recall it the next morning. It helps keep balance in my life as well, since I can physically see at a glance how I spent my week – after the fact. Writing things down provides us with a sort of immortality.

**Choosing a planner**

Here are five things that an effective planning calendar should include.

1. A place to record your goals since they are an integral part of the planning process.

2. A place to record your mission statement as well since it reminds you of why you your purpose in life and forms the launching pad for your goals.

3. Each day broken into 15 minute increments, including Saturdays and Sundays as well as evenings to facilitate the scheduling of personal as well as business projects and activities.

4. Daily follow-up sections to record deadlines for assignments due, birthdays and other special events, and notes reminding you when to check the follow-up file.

5. Weekly and daily "To Do" sections to record non-priority items that should be done.

Your planner is the most important time management and life management tool, so choose it carefully. For a description and view of the *Taylor Planner*, which I designed over 30 years ago, visit our website at taylorintime.com. There are hundreds of planners on the market, including electronic calendars and Apps. Select one that you will feel comfortable using, and use it.

**Make a commitment, not a "To Do" list**

A "To Do" list is a basic form of planning inasmuch as it reminds us of all the things we want to do in the future. Unfortunately, working exclusively from a "To Do" list is like using a manual typewriter for your word processing. It is simply not adequate in today's environment of speed, complexity and busyness. For one thing, "To Do" lists are only one-dimensional; they tell you all the things you want to do and nothing more. They fail to take into consideration that you may not have time to do them all or that some of them are more important than others or that a few with them may not even be worth doing. If you went a step further, and prioritized the list, and scheduled time for the high priority items in your planner, you would have a higher level of planning. Although a "To Do" list is a rudimentary form of planning; scheduling is planning expressing itself as action. Scheduled activities are three-dimensional; they tell you what you have to do, when you are going to do them, and how long they are expected to take. Also, if something is scheduled, you know it's a priority. Things that are left on your "To Do" list are either postponed or die a natural death. "To do" lists are intentions; but scheduled blocks of time in your planner are commitments. "To Do" lists are endless and can get longer by the day. But those things scheduled in your planner are finite; they have a starting time, a working time (with a built-in allowance for interruptions) and a definite ending time. Items that are scheduled usually get done; items on a "To do" list are usually delayed. And what's delayed is frequently abandoned.

**Balance high-tech with high-touch**

Why would I ever use a paper planner in a world of digital technology? Balancing high-tech with high-touch can strengthen "executive skills, and technology writer Danny O'Brien interviewed top achievers and found one thing in common that may account for their increased productivity. They all used some sort low-tech tool, such as a written "To Do" list or a plain paper pad.

In addition to the planner I use a hard copy *Telephone & E-mail Log* in which to make notes when I talk to people on the telephone or review my email. I find more people are using this as we get further into the digital age – probably because it prevents multitasking while on the telephone, improves concentration, shows co-workers you are actually busy and not available to them, and most important, insures that you don't forget that you have to do something as you switch from call to call and interruption to interruption. I'm not advocating a return to paperwork; but I do advocate the merging of high-tech and high-touch. There should be no embarrassment in using paperwork when it actually serves you better and improves your efficiency. It's even more important to have an organized mind than an organized working environment – although they do complement each other.

The *Caveman Principle* , as explained by Michio Kaku, professor of theoretical physics at the City College and City University of New York, says that given a choice between high-tech and high-touch, we opt for high-touch every time. For example, would you rather see a celebrity performer sing at a concert or watch a DVD of the same performance? Or how about a live sporting even vs. a re-run on TV? Perhaps that's why some predictions about the future were wrong – such as the "paperless office." There is actually more paper since the advent of computers. People trust concrete evidence more than they do electrons on a computer screen that disappear when you turn off the screen. That's probably another reason I still prefer to use a paper planner.

# CONTROL YOUR BRAIN

**Increase your focus in spite of interruptions**

Most of us are ill-equipped to deal with the onslaught of interruptions introduced by technology. Our brain's natural inclination is to react to them. We coped with this in the old days by isolating ourselves from interruptions – by closing our office door and having our calls screened or intercepted – or by going to a coffee shop where no one could contact us. With the advent of the smartphone, e-mail, texting and portable devices, interruptions now follow us wherever we go. We are at the mercy of our own ability or inability to resist the urge to answer our smart phones, check incoming e-mail or respond to text messages. Removing the source of temptation could involve turning off your handheld devices while you work on priority projects, and keeping the paperwork, to do lists and other distractions out of sight while working on a specific task, and leaving your cell phone at home if you decide to work in a coffee shop. You could also do all your priority work in the same place – one devoid of distracting scenery, pictures or paraphernalia so your brain gets to associate that space with work. Resisting temptation might involve not going online or replying to e-mail before 10 a.m., ignoring a ringing telephone when you're talking with family and friends, and resisting any urge to buy electronic devices that you really don't need. (After all, who really needs a smart watch when they already have a smart phone? It's much more important to have a smart brain.) But even if you could block out all external distractions, you would still have to contend with your tendency to interrupt yourself and let your mind wander and daydream. It is a function of our "reactive brain," which is always on the alert for unusual or sudden motion, sound or sightings. It's a built-in safety factor for our own good. After all, regardless of what you are doing, you wouldn't want to ignore a threatening shadow appearing in your peripheral vision. Depending on your level of interest in the task and its duration and complexity, you will always have a few distractions that you cannot avoid. Accept them, and don't sweat the small stuff. But continual distractions, either internal or external, that seriously impede your personal productivity, must be eliminated. And they can be. The Gorilla Experiment, originally conducted about 18 years ago, and described in the 2009 book, *The Invisible Gorilla*, involved subjects watching a video of two teams of three people passing a basketball back and forth among their team members. A person dressed in a gorilla suit walked onto the playing court during the exercise, paused for a few seconds, and then walked away. Before showing them the video, the subjects were asked to count the number of passes made by the team wearing the white shirts and to ignore any passes made by the team in the black shirts. The psychologists showed the same video to everyone. Half the viewers never noticed the gorilla.

They coined the phrase "illusion of attention" to describe the fact that we are unaware of how much we are really missing in our visual world. But it also illustrates that if we are focusing intensely on a task or project, we are able to ignore interruptions or potential distractions – even if they are within our field of vision. Self-discipline or self-control, focus, attention, and planning are essential if we are to remain effective in this digital age of speed. These are all functions of our executive center in the prefrontal cortex area of our brain. If the executive skills, such as sustained attention, controlling impulses and goal-directed persistence are weak, you will find it difficult to concentrate. The ability to focus is one of the most critical brain functions according to Barbara Strauch, author of *The secret life of the grown-up brain* That's why I claim that the battlefield has shifted from the office to the brain, and why it is so important to strengthen our brain-based executive skills. But how do we strengthen these skills and ignore the beckoning distractions?

**You can ignore distractions and break bad habits**

if there's anything worse than being a slave to technology, it's being a slave to your own brain. We are at times the victims of our own habits, and find ourselves doing things we really don't want to do. Some people have a harder time focusing, while others have a harder time ignoring distractions. Our ability to willfully focus attention is physically separate from our ability to ignore distractions vying for our attention. Earl Miller, a neuroscientist at MIT, led a 2007 study that discovered that willful concentration and unintentional attention are not the same, and are not controlled by the same region of the brain. In either case, you can change your brain. Your brain simply responds to how it has been wired – either by you, others, or circumstances. You are not what you are; you are what you decide you will be. You – or at least your mind – must take control. If you don't, your brain takes control by default. It switches to autopilot, based on the original course it was programmed to follow. We are hardwired to always default to fast-paced shifts in focus. Jeffrey Schwartz and Rebecca Gladding, authors of the book, *You are not your brain* , say that the mind's ability to change the brain is referred to as self-directed neuroplasticity. They claim that your mind can veto any action taken habitually by the brain. So gaining control of your technology and your life requires taking control of your brain through self-directed neuroplasticity.

**Strengthen your executive skills**

Research shows that the Internet and digital technology can have a negative impact on our ability to learn, focus, pay attention, memorize and relate to others on a personal basis. It can also gobble up our time, encourage busyness and multi-tasking and stifle creativity. With strong executive skills, however, you can more effectively resist the incessant interruptions and distractions of today's environment, focus on your important tasks, and continue to get the important things done. Sometimes referred to as "habits of the mind", a person's "executive skills" are those brain-based skills required to execute tasks – that is, getting organized, planning, initiating work, staying on task, controlling impulses, regulating emotions, and being adaptable and resilient – the very skills needed to stay focused and productive in today's environment. Your energy, willpower and mental strength will increase as you get adequate sleep, exercise and diet, manage stress well, and balance high-tech with high touch, remain socially active, control your working environment and manage the technology in your life. But there is one missing ingredient – motivation.

**Motivation is all in your mind**

Researchers have already shown that musicians, athletes and others can expand the brain areas associated with those skills by mental activity alone. The brain can also change in response to messages generated internally by our thoughts and intentions. The problem is it takes effort. For neuroplasticity to work, you'll have to stick with the new behavior until you can do it effortlessly. Practice until it becomes a habit. By considering possibilities instead of limitations on a regular basis, you'll rewire your brain. You can train yourself to change the way you think. The key is to get started, which means doing what you don't feel like doing and continuing to do it. To do this you will have to overcome the initial inertia, which requires motivation. Motivation is a critical component of neuroplasticity. You must want to change, and believe that it's possible to change, before you can actually change.

That's how placebos work. Patients want to get well. Their desire to get well is strong. And since they think that they are taking a new drug that will help them, the expectancy that it will work is high. Motivation is the product of desire and expectancy.

Someone who is disorganized, for example, can become organized if they willingly buy into a routine of practising organizing principles again and again with the expectancy that it will help them become organized. F or habits to permanently change, people must believe that change is feasible. When people come together to help one another change, that belief becomes even stronger. So in forming any new habit, it is usually easier to do so when you have the support and encouragement of others.

You are not what you are; you are what you decide you will be.

# ABOUT THE AUTHOR

Harold Mawela is an inspirational speaker, coach, writer, teacher, providing effective, practical, down-to-earth advice based on his own leadership experience and the application of relevant leadership thinking.

As a trainer and coach, Harold's focus is simply to help people maximize their potential better by helping them develop their selfconfidence and equipping them with the necessary skills and behaviors to up their game.

The advice that Harold is able to share with his clients is based on his own leadership and management experience, he is able to offer insights into best practice and to draw on the experiences of others as to what works and what doesn't.

www.ingramcontent.com/pod-product-compliance
Lightning Source LLC
Chambersburg PA
CBHW030612220526
45463CB00004B/1272